CW01024605

Praise for U[illegible]
Transform you[illegible] profitability thr[illegible] of productivity in just 100 days

Amanda redefines the 4P's to drive productivity with a comprehensive look at people, promise, price and process, all key to business in a changing world. If you are seeking a book that explores the subject and want to be inspired by a far deeper understanding of what makes for improved productivity, then this is most certainly one to read. Packed full of insight and practical applications it will help you make sense of the subject and create a productive culture.

Barnaby Wynter, Master Brand Creation Expert and MBA facilitator, Author of Become the Go-to Brand

Having written several books on personal and team productivity, I have always been aware that there is a bigger game at play – organisational productivity. How do you unblock the barriers that get in the way of the overall productivity and output of your organisation? In *Unblock*, Amanda Sokell suggests that it starts with measurement, and provides some simple ways for your leaders to work out where their team is at with productivity, and where they need to be. She then explores how productive cultures can create the environment where productivity is an automatic outcome of how the team works. As a business leader, a part of your role is to improve the productivity of your team and organisation. Read this to fast-track how you do that.

Dermot Crowley, Author of Smart Work, Smart Teams *and* Lead Smart

Some 20 years ago, as Chair of a couple of Vistage groups I was wise enough to persuade Amanda to join. Whilst my task was to 'challenge' Amanda, I found, as I worked with her, that we were rapidly moving towards role reversal!

Having read *Unblock* I now know that the growth I observed in Amanda's thinking, precise, analytical and logical, has progressed exponentially.

Unblock is essential reading for any CEO seriously invested in increasing productivity. It covers all the critical areas – Managing Change, Pricing, People, Culture and Managing Intellectual Lethargy. I specifically related to her approach of providing multiple case studies, ranging from local motorbike dealers to Global brands, to illustrate key points. Facts tell: Stories sell.

Amanda's background reading and research is comprehensive, professional and well laid out. Her 'tools' are dynamic and useful, her thinking precise and persuasive and her book a "must read".

Chris Hughes, Emeritus Vistage Chair

I have always believed simplicity is the end point of understanding. *Unblock* is a book which delivers just that. Amanda has managed to condense the whole spectrum of business strategy, key business success factors and the drivers of productivity into a highly readable book. Her success in achieving this is the result of many years as a practitioner rather than as an academic. I would recommend this book to any business owner or senior manager who is trying to find a cohesive explanation of productivity and how to deliver it across the whole business.

Roger Martin-Fagg, Behavioural Economist

Working with Amanda supercharged my business in its early stages. Since then I have devoured everything she has produced. Strongly recommend others do exactly the same by reading this book.

Phil Turner, Former CEO, Philharmonic AV

Unblock is a must read for anyone seeking to understand productivity challenges. Amanda Sokell brilliantly unravels the complexities of post-2008 productivity stagnation, offering practical solutions for businesses and leaders. The detailed analysis of problematic versus systematic cultures provides pragmatic strategies to shift any organisation towards peak productivity. Sokell's insights are not only timely but essential for driving growth in today's economy.

Ishan Galapathy, Author of Hidden Growth Opportunities, Advance and Unlock

In a rapidly changing world, driven by the accelerated disruption of the workplace, workforce and marketplace, all powered by the relentless advance of technology, CEOs must focus on improving the productivity levers within their control to get more from their organization. *Unblock* creates a clear thought framework for defining and driving productivity with strategies, tactics and pathways to deliver the organizational change required to become measurably more productive.

Joe Galvin, Chief Research Officer, Vistage International

In *Unblock* Amanda Sokell provides a roadmap for business leaders determined to make productivity a core part of their organisation's DNA. Drawing on real-world examples and a deep understanding of the challenges businesses face today, she lays out practical steps that any company can take to unlock its full potential. This book is a crucial resource for those of us committed to driving the UK's productivity forward, one business at a time.

Anthony Impey, Chief Executive, Be the Business

UNBLOCK

Transform your company's profitability through a culture of productivity in just 100 days

With best wishes A

amanda sokell

First published in Great Britain by Practical Inspiration Publishing, 2024

© Amanda Sokell, 2024

The moral rights of the author have been asserted

ISBN	9781788606967	(hardback)
	9781788606974	(paperback)
	9781788606998	(epub)
	9781788606981	(mobi)

All rights reserved. This book, or any portion thereof, may not be reproduced without the express written permission of the author.

Every effort has been made to trace copyright holders and to obtain their permission for the use of copyright material. The publisher apologizes for any errors or omissions and would be grateful if notified of any corrections that should be incorporated in future reprints or editions of this book.

Want to bulk-buy copies of this book for your team and colleagues? We can customize the content and co-brand *Unblock* to suit your business's needs.

Please email info@practicalinspiration.com for more details.

To Ian, Alex & Felix, my reasons for being

Contents

Preface xi

Introduction 1

Part 1 – Productivity Cultures 17

Your Productivity Culture 19

Part 2 – Improving Productivity 39

Productivity Drivers 41

Promise 45

Price 63

People 87

Process 111

Part 3 – Finding Untapped Productivity 141

Conducting an Unblock Audit™ 143

Part 4 – Solutions 169

Which Lever to Pull? 171

Prioritization 183

Change Management 195

Summary 213

Acknowledgements 217

Bibliography 221

Index 233

Preface

I have spent my entire working life making change, finding ways to redesign, optimize or restructure organizations' operations. I seem to have an unusual ability to get under the skin of an organization in a very short time and work out what makes it tick. Some have described this as my superpower.

In a career that has spanned marketing, sales, software development, training and consultancy across a wide range of industries, including public relations (PR), insurance, telecommunications, manufacturing, design, retail, pharmaceuticals and financial services, I have found myself looking at the organization and asking: why do you do it that way?

All too often, I have been involved in relatively isolated projects to improve an aspect of the organization, which, although worthy, have ignored a range of other factors that are essential to improving the outcomes of the organization.

Most of this work has had at its core a desire to improve productivity, and yet, rarely, if ever, has the organization's productivity been measured before the project took place and again afterwards to validate the desired improvement.

One could go as far as to say that I have never come across an organization that accurately measures and manages its productivity at an organizational level. Yes, there have been companies that bill time and focus on utilization or manufacturing companies that monitor output from their production lines. However, these only ever measure part of the total organization's productivity and are, therefore, flawed.

When beginning to look at this topic, I found libraries full of productivity books. There is something for everyone, from time management to inbox zero, prioritization, delegation, mindset, you name it. But could I find a single book that looked at the interrelated aspects of an organization's productivity, those things that dictate its productivity culture and, therefore, its ability to improve its productivity? In short, no.

Having worked on numerous apparently successful projects that, at best, delivered marginal gain compared to the intended return on investment, I have become jaded by projects, frequently software implementations, that fail to deliver promised returns because they are looked at in isolation without understanding that the neuroscience of our brains means this is almost certainly setting them up to underdeliver.

Unblock is my attempt to provide an alternative perspective. It sets out why measuring productivity is important and, most crucially, how to do it for your whole organization, no matter what industry you operate within. It then outlines the four levers that drive productivity, understanding, of course, that within any system they will be interrelated. And then, for those who wish to adopt my philosophy, there is practical advice on how to understand your starting point, prioritize the improvements you identify and manage the ensuing change.

Supporting resources are referenced throughout and can be found at my website 👆 https://resources.amandasokell.com.

It introduces some new concepts that will hopefully one day become useful and recognized metrics in every board pack: the productivity wage quotient (PWQ) and the order integrity ratio (OIR).

This book is written first and foremost for business leaders, with whom rests the responsibility and accountability to improve productivity within their various organizations. I hope it provides a useful insight into why so much of what you might have done in the past has proved hard work.

And to the academics, economists and policymakers who pick this up, perhaps we can start a new conversation about productivity and, more importantly, how we might create the macroeconomic environment, including defining fiscal policy to help improve it.

Introduction

The productivity puzzle

Since the financial crisis of 2008 the UK in particular has struggled to improve its productivity. Before 2008 the UK's long-term productivity growth was a steady 2.3% per year.[1] Even after the recessions of 1980/81 and 1990/91, when productivity growth was temporarily reduced, once the recession was over, the rate of productivity growth reverted to the long-term trend.[2]

For some reason 2008 was different. Productivity growth dropped and since has averaged a mere 0.4% to 2023 Q1.[3] This phenomenon has become known as the 'productivity puzzle' and has been the subject of much debate. The Government has even set up a programme, 'Be the Business',

---

1 (Office for National Statistics 2024)

2 (Wikipedia – UK Recessions n.d.)

3 (Office for National Statistics 2024)

led by a range of industry leaders.[4] This organization runs programmes that share information on how to boost productivity to improve the UK's productivity growth.

Despite the positive impact of organizations like 'Be the Business', and a wider focus on productivity growth over many years, productivity rates have not significantly increased across the country.

Be the Business

The Government launched the industry-led programme 'Be the Business' to help small businesses adopt best practices. In 2015, then-Prime Minister David Cameron commissioned a review of the UK's ongoing productivity challenges. This review, supported by some of the country's leading business people, found that the UK productivity situation could be improved by increasing the management skills of business leaders and accelerating investment in certain technologies.

Be the Business is funded and supported by the UK Government and several large companies, including GSK, Siemens, Amazon, BAE Systems, McKinsey & Co. and Accenture. It runs several leadership and mentoring programmes designed to help small businesses improve their skills.

---

[4] (Be The Business n.d.)

What is productivity?

What do we mean by productivity?

When we talk about productivity, we refer to 'labour productivity'. In other words, the value of goods and services produced per quantity of labour used to create them. Essentially, productivity is, therefore, a financial metric. Many organizations use productivity metrics such as units per hour; however, this generally measures only one part of a business, whereas the productivity that concerns us here is the productivity of the entire system or company.

The value of goods and services is not as simple as the turnover. We need to identify the value added that is generated by an organization's labour force. In the UK and in many other countries, we are familiar with VAT (Value Added Tax) as a tax on the value added by an organization within the supply chain. To calculate the value of tax due, we take the value of our outputs (sales) and deduct the value of our inputs (purchases), thereby calculating the value added by each party within the supply chain.

It is worth noting that the US is one of the only developed countries in the world that does not have a VAT system. Instead it uses a sales tax system administered by the individual states. This sales tax is not applied at each supply chain step, rather it is a consumption tax applied at the end when a product or service is sold to the end customer.

Value added, in the context of productivity, is precisely the same as within the VAT system – it is the value created (added) by an organization and, therefore, is calculated by taking an organization's annual turnover and deducting all the expenses paid for on invoices. It is essential to ensure that only invoice payments are deducted – wages and salaries are not to be included in this calculation. One way to get to this number quickly is to look at net profit before tax and then add depreciation, wages and salaries. This figure is known as gross value added, or GVA.

To convert this to a productivity measure, we need to divide this figure by the number of employees or the total hours worked. I use the number of employees because this results in a productivity value per employee and can easily be compared with average salary numbers. A rough and ready calculation can be undertaken by doing a headcount; however, with part-time workers, joiners and leavers, and in some cases paid overtime, it is better to do an accurate FTE (full-time equivalent) calculation before settling on a number.

If you want to calculate your productivity using this method, check out the tool available at 👆 https://resources.amandasokell.com.

In March 2024 the mean average wage in the UK was £34,900.[5&6] It is worth calculating your organization's average mean salary and comparing it with your productivity number. If your productivity figure is less than your mean average salary, your organization will be operating at a loss. If productivity is more than the mean average salary, it will be making a profit or surplus.

---

5 (Thornhill and Howard 2024)

6 (Office for National Statistics (ONS) 2024)

A critical quotient that is helpful to monitor is productivity : mean average wage which I have called the productivity wage quotient (PWQ). So, if your productivity is £35,000 and you have a mean average salary of £34,900, your PWQ is 1.002.

$$productivy\ wage\ quotient = \frac{£35,000}{£34,900} = 1.002$$

The larger this figure, the better.

If the PWQ is less than 1, it indicates that your organization will likely be making a loss; in fact, all the value generated is for the workforce. If the PWQ is larger than 1, some value generated as a surplus or for shareholders. The higher the PWQ, the more value is available for shareholders, higher wages or reinvestment.

Productivity growth is calculated as a percentage change over time. For example, if your productivity at the end of Q1 in any given year is £31,876 and your productivity at the end of Q2 of the same year is £32,000, your productivity growth for the quarter would be 0.4%

$$productivity\ growth = \frac{(£32,000\text{-}£31,876)}{£31,876} \times 100 = 0.4\%$$

A word on charities

I am often asked how all this relates to charities. After all, profit tends to be a dirty word in the not-for-profit world. The calculation for a charity is identical to any other organization.

One of the ways a charity creates value is by galvanizing a host of volunteers to deliver its services. In the productivity calculation, this 'labour' is free of charge as it commands no salary and is excluded in the FTE calculation. For charities, as in other organizations, the only people to include are those on the payroll.

Charity income includes all income from any source, whether fundraising, grants, trading or donations.

Behind the headline numbers

The top-level numbers for the whole economy are, of course, an aggregation of the productivity growth of all the companies in the UK. So, is it realistic to assume that there is uniformity of growth across the board?

Unsurprisingly, the answer to this is no. I have been tracking the productivity of clients I work with for many years. I have seen that no matter what the industry or the company's size, there are companies with good productivity and others with poor productivity. Whether you have five to ten or 5,000 employees, you can have industry-beating productivity, or your productivity can be well below the UK average. It does not matter whether you are in manufacturing, the knowledge sector or retail – the same applies. The only sector so far where I have found an anomaly is the banking sector, where productivity figures are significantly higher (by a factor of ten or more) than other industries.

Broader research reflects my data:

> '... *the evidence suggests that our high and low productivity businesses vary greatly in size and the problem is just as*

> *likely up and down the size range. The plain fact is that two thirds of our workforce is employed in businesses with productivity below the industry average: whichever businesses they are working in, their work is not as productive as it might be elsewhere.'*[7]

Across industries, there will be reasons why productivity may have slowed down. The financial sector saw a significant drop in the aftermath of the financial crisis of 2008, and increased regulation certainly had an impact. The construction industry also saw a sharp downturn when borrowing became far more challenging. However, other industries that have continued to grow, such as technology and communications, have also seen a sharp decline in productivity growth.

Every industry sector has seen a decrease in productivity growth since 2008. Despite this, in each industry there are a few companies that are outperforming the market. Those organizations, which push the boundaries of what others might accept as possible, have continued to see productivity growth similar to what they experienced before the recession of 2008. Such organizations continue to improve how they work, presumably faster than 2.3% per annum, because when calculating the long-term average, the many companies making no progress are reducing the average.

The root cause

The UK's 'productivity puzzle' has been the topic of significant research and writing for more than 15 years since the 2008

[7] (Productivity Leadership Group 2016)

recession. Consequently, there have been many underlying reasons cited. Let's take a look at some of these.

Skills gap and education

The UK Government has conducted an employer skills survey every two years since 2011. The most recent survey is dated 2022, a slight gap since the previous pre-Covid report of 2019.

This skills survey aims to track how employers manage a skilled labour force across the UK, and represents a large-scale telephone survey that in 2022 included 72,918 employers across the UK.[8] The survey highlights some concerning trends in employer training and education.

Percentage of establishments that have funded or arranged any training for staff over the past 12 months

60%

A decrease from 66% in 2017.

For example, the 2022 survey identified that 60% of employers have funded or arranged training for staff within the past 12 months. This compares to 66% in 2017. When we consider the rate of change in the world over these five years, how technology has changed, how we work has changed, and the changes brought about by the Covid pandemic, it is unsettling to see that the number of organizations implementing staff training has declined. How can our workers possibly hope to keep up with new technology and ways of working if they are not trained in how to do so?

8 (Department for Education 2023)

This statistic is particularly sobering when compared with others. For example, the skill-shortage vacancy density (the number of vacancies that are proving difficult to fill due to the establishment not being able to find applicants with the appropriate skills, qualifications or experience as a proportion of all vacancies) increased from 22% in 2017 to 36% in the 2022 survey, while the percentage of organizations with at least one skill-shortage vacancy grew from 6% to 10% over the same period.

Skill-shortage vacancy density (SSVs as a share of vacancies)

36%

An increase from 22% in 2017.

Percentage of establishments with at least one skill-shortage vacancy

10%

An increase from 6% in 2017.

Lack of investment in technology

When we look back at significant step changes in our productivity, it almost always coincides with a change of tools resulting from an investment in technology. The scythe dates back to 500 BC and may have been used in Ancient Rome. By the 8th century, it was more common across Europe for mowing hay and, by the 16th century had become the preferred tool for reaping crops, replacing the sickle. It was ergonomically comfortable and efficient as a tool for reaping crops. However, it required a considerable amount of manual labour to bring in a harvest this way.

In the early 1800s we saw the first versions of the modern combine harvester, which was patented in the US.[9] It and many early versions were horse-drawn and required 20 horses to pull them. While the combine harvester improved productivity by combining three operations into one (reaping, threshing and winnowing), it still required a significant input in terms of horse-drawn power.

By the late 1800s and early 1900s, motorized vehicles were beginning to take the place of horse-drawn machines. An engine does not have vet bills or need feeding and stabling, and certainly, in some parts of the world, is not as susceptible to heat. So the move towards mechanized farm production continued. Today we see solitary farmers cutting acres of fields with a single machine that spits out tightly bound bales in its wake.

It is a lesson in how to effect a step-change in productivity. Farmers achieved significant productivity gains when they changed their tools and invested in technology. There are only so many ways to train somebody with a scythe to become more productive.

When we look towards modern business, our tools are frequently the contemporary equivalent of the scythe. In a world where the pace of change is so fast, it no longer takes centuries for new tools that drive better productivity to emerge. Yet the tools a business uses are updated infrequently and often way past their sell-by date.

There is a comfort in the tools we use. They can become like a trusty scythe with a hand-worn handle that fits comfortably

---

9 (Plant Planet 2021)

in the grasp. Unfortunately, our current tools, like a scythe, will not help us increase our productivity.

A UK-focused 2018 paper by the McKinsey Global Institute found that equipment investment as a share of value added declined by 20% before and after the 2008 financial crisis, with 50% of the decline coming from manufacturing.[10]

Management practices

Several studies have looked at the correlation between management practices and productivity. In 2017 a collaboration between the Economic Statistics Centre of Excellence and the Office for National Statistics (ONS) conducted the 'Management and Expectations Survey', which aimed to measure management practices using a broad set of metrics across a wide range of industries, including both manufacturing and services industries. They identified a statistically significant correlation between management practice scores and productivity. They found that a 0.1 increase (on a scale of 0 to 1) in the score they devised for management practices is associated with a 9.6% increase in productivity. The UK's productivity growth has been less than 1% per year since 2008, so a 9.6% increase is significant.

The survey found that structured management practices are more likely to be present in service industries than in production industries, among foreign-owned firms rather than UK-owned firms, and in non-family-owned businesses rather than family-owned firms. High levels of employment

---

[10] (McKinsey Global Institute 2018)

(larger organizations) also contributed to more structured management practices.

Structured management practices they defined include:

- Continuous improvement practices – the way a firm monitors its operations and uses the information for continuous improvement
- Key performance indicators (KPIs) – how many KPIs are tracked and how often they are reviewed
- Targets – whether targets are stretching, tracked and appropriately reviewed
- Employment practices – whether employees are promoted and rewarded based on performance, whether under-performance is managed, and whether there are adequate training opportunities
- Organizational practices – how decentralized decision-making is

A copy of the questions that comprised the survey can be found on the ONS website at Annex 1.[11] The overall score is a simple average of the scores across all questions. The average score of the 2017 survey population was 0.49.

Macroeconomic factors

Other factors that are considered to impact the productivity of an economy include:

- Infrastructure issues
- Regional disparities
- Demographic factors

---

[11] (Office for National Statistics (ONS) 2018)

- Policy and regulatory environment

While these elements undoubtedly play a role in productivity growth, or lack thereof, they are primarily macroeconomic factors rather than ones that an individual business can control. Given this is a book about what companies can do to increase productivity, the easiest route is to look at the factors within their control first, so these macroeconomic factors will not be the focus.

The possible exception to this is demographic factors, whereby an organization, while somewhat at the mercy of the global trend of an ageing population, can control its demographics when measured by other criteria, including gender, race and neurodiversity.

Change

As the Greek philosopher Heraclitus is quoted as saying:

'Change is the only constant in life.'

To improve productivity, we need to change how we work.

Sadly, as human beings, we find change remarkably difficult. While some people relish change and are constantly innovating, improving and, in some cases, causing chaos for their colleagues with their constant desire to improve things, the vast majority of us quite like the status quo. Even when we say we are fed up with the status quo, when it comes down to it we are incredibly reluctant to change our established habits. I have lost count of the number of times I have worked with a team that is 'desperate' for a better way of working and, when it comes down to making and implementing the required changes, somehow finds that change is a good idea when it applies to everyone else, provided they can continue to work in precisely the same way.

So, if improving productivity requires change, then it is also about change management. While a lack of investment in technology, a lack of training, poor management practices, or any of the issues commonly cited are factors, one common element that sits beneath all of them, hampering our desire for change, is our innately human condition of *lethargy*.

I see lethargy as a disease that is often linked to forgetfulness. It gradually permeates the culture of organizations until even obviously unproductive processes are tolerated because the alternative requires too much effort. Every time I work with an organization to improve its productivity, I uncover all manner of work practices being endured, even though those undertaking them know they are inherently inefficient.

In many ways, it is a bit like those of us for whom a car is something to get us from A to B. Its inner workings are not of much interest. When the service is due, it is a chore to sort out; if the windscreen wash runs out, it is not a high priority to top up. Air in the tyres, checking the oil? Can I really be bothered when I have so many other things to juggle in life? So, while the car continues to get me from A to B, it is not running as smoothly, the spark plugs may be misfiring, the tyres are wearing more quickly than they should and it is consuming more fuel than necessary. My lethargy for car maintenance is reducing its productivity.

Neuroscience shows us that, at the level of the brain, lethargy is the result of the brain's natural predisposition to conserve energy. It will be delighted if it can get through the day without doing any real thinking. Instead, it would prefer to use patterns and predictions to help us function rather than the hard work of 'thinking'. A study in 2018 by Matthieu Boisgontier of the University of British Columbia suggests that our brains may be wired to prefer lying on the couch.[12] Essentially, our brains are naturally lethargic.

Lethargy

Suppose we reconsider the most-cited reasons for our productivity puzzle or low productivity growth. We can see that lethargy is at the root of all of them.

Skills gap and education

Underneath these headlines of lack of training or skills shortages lies lethargy. From the employer's perspective, perhaps identifying skills gaps and organizing training is simply too much like hard work; or from an employee's perspective, perhaps learning new things is too challenging and disruptive.

Lack of investment in technology

Researching, understanding, selecting, implementing and training everyone on new technology is understandably a big job, particularly with an ageing workforce where technology adoption can be more of a challenge. It is often easier to

[12] (Boisgontier, et al. 2018)

become distracted by other priorities and put this in the 'too hard' box – lethargy in action.

Management practices

The proportion of business management undertaking any self-development is reported to be low. In the UK, a Chartered Management Institute study found that 82% of those who enter management positions have no formal management training,[13] and in the US, research by Dr Jack Wiley indicates that over 70% have had no management training or it was capped at four hours.[14] If our leaders are not investing in themselves, they may be unaware of the management practices that could help improve productivity. It is a lot like the effort involved in getting to the gym: lethargy kicks in, so nothing happens.

We even train our team members to be lethargic when we repeatedly discount their suggestions.

13 (Chartered Management Institute 2023)

14 (Wiley 2023)

Part 1

Productivity Cultures

Your Productivity Culture

Having worked with organizations of all shapes and sizes over the last two decades, I have noticed four dominant cultures that determine the productivity of the entire organization. Two of these cultures are dominated by pervading lethargy, while the other two are characterized by productivity.

We can usually get a good indication of the productivity culture of an organization using the PWQ calculated by dividing an organization's productivity by its mean average salary. However, this needs to be considered in conjunction with the types of behaviours exhibited by the organization to truly understand which culture applies.

The culture of an organization is concerned with the behaviours that operate within it. As Jim Whitehurst writes in his article on culture for the *Harvard Business Review*:

> *'For me, organizational culture is defined by how people inside the organization interact with each other. Culture is learned behaviour – it's not a by-product of operations. It's not an overlay. We create our organizational culture by the actions we take; not the other way around.'*[15]

---

[15] (Whitehurst 2016)

Recognizing that we are concerned with behaviours and that behaviours define organizational culture, it naturally follows that the current culture will be defined by the way in which team members behave, and whether this is inherently lethargic or productive.

Let's take a look in detail at these four cultures.

Problematic

We will look first at the problematic culture, since this is the one where many organizations operate week to week, year to year.

In numeric terms, a problematic culture exists where the PWQ falls between 1 and around 1.7.

If we are walking around such organizations, what behaviours might we encounter?

We define a problem as a negative deviation from our 'normal'. It is common for all organizations to experience problems occasionally; however, in a problematic culture, we might expect it to exhibit deviations from the normal or problems on a regular basis.

When a problem occurs, typically, we see team members engaged in 'fixing the problem'. Investigations arise and steps are taken to prevent the problem from reoccurring. If the issues did not exist, all this energy could be redirected to delivering value and contributing to productive endeavours. Instead, it is consumed by putting right things that have gone wrong or have not gone to plan.

As a business grows, the owner/founder becomes increasingly distant from the operational activities; things they might once have spotted go undetected. The same problem may occur regularly, or the expected behaviour might, in fact, be a problem. In problematic organizations the standard behaviour line has dropped; although team members know what they are doing is not sensible, because it is expected, they do not think to mention or change it.

A problematic culture is a little like problematic skin. When a teenager suffers from acne, we consider it the norm for all teenagers and pay little attention. Many teenagers suffer from severe acne, unaware there are treatments they can use to minimize the effects, such as antibiotics and other more potent therapies.

It is often the same in problematic cultures. Team members may need clarification about how to do things or who does what. Training may be ad hoc on the job rather than formalized. Information can be 'lost' as successive employees transfer knowledge to recruits; a further part of the original working practice being lost each time.

Lethargy pervades within problematic cultures. We are all guilty of this at times. The problem must frequently be more significant to warrant the short-term pain required to realize the long-term gain.

My mobile phone is an excellent example. Recently, fingerprint recognition ceased to work. To unlock my phone I had to enter the PIN code. Despite the inconvenience, the effort to pause and retrain my phone to recognize my fingerprint was too much to overcome the inertia of the problem. The adverse effect was not significant enough to overcome my lethargy and fix it.

Case study: Glazing manufacturer

An aluminium window company was frustrated that its lead times were increasing and it was becoming less able to meet customer requirements. The production delays resulted in more work-in-progress on the factory floor. These part-finished orders were increasingly at risk of damage as they waited between stations for the next part of the manufacturing process to be completed. When damage occurred, the order needed to be returned to a previous stage in the process and the damage corrected.

The lethargy stemmed from a belief that it took six weeks for an order to complete, and it was not possible to do it any faster. This status quo had not been challenged and, consequently, processes and systems were established around this assumption. After looking in detail at how orders were being fulfilled, I challenged this concept, which sparked ideas on eliminating the work-in-progress, minimizing potential damage and reducing lead times for all customers.

I have been lucky to learn the art of creative facilitation from David Hall of the Ideas Centre.[16] In one of our sessions he

[16] (David Hall n.d.)

explained how difficult it is for humans to see beyond our world of 'what is'. The pattern systems in our brains mean that we often see what our brain expects to be there. He shared the following case study, which indicates a problematic culture and demonstrates the benefit of a structured problem-solving approach.

Case study: Laboratory

A laboratory used a range of glass beakers, test tubes and flasks daily during its operations. These were cleaned every evening and ready for use the next day. The cleaning was performed in a high-temperature dishwasher in an adjacent building, and the contract cleaning staff were responsible for cleaning and replacing the glass equipment every evening.

When a new financial director joined the organization, they were surprised at the budget size for replacing glass. Upon investigation they discovered that the glass equipment was frequently broken during the cleaning process. Due to the regular daily influx of significant numbers of samples for analysis, and with time of the essence, the lab had historically arranged with a local glass supplier to replace broken glassware on the same day as reported, at a considerable regular cost.

This status quo had been going on for years. This problematic issue was accepted as the 'normal' way of working; glass gets broken during cleaning, and more needs to be purchased, quickly.

Thanks to the challenge provided by the new financial director and a structured problem-solving session using a creative facilitation technique, the organization reviewed the processes and discovered that moving the equipment from one location to another was the most likely time for it to break. By installing dishwashing facilities in each lab and making the scientists responsible for cleaning their equipment, breakages and the budget were reduced significantly.

Organizations can often survive for years with problematic cultures. While they are not delivering serious levels of profit or surplus, they are also not making a loss, so there can be little motivation to work hard to change things. This culture likely permeates most of the UK economy, contributing to poor productivity growth. A good place for such organizations to start is to focus on quality, looking for and eradicating quality issues wherever they are found.

The danger for these organizations is that now and then, they are affected by a significant event, and to be able to deal with it they need a different culture or large reserves. Such events may be internally driven, such as the loss of a critical member of staff or a key client; or externally driven, such as an economic downturn, a change of government legislation or, heaven forbid, a pandemic. When this occurs, the organization's culture can quickly fall into what I call a 'traumatic' culture.

Traumatic

Trauma manifests in two main ways – physical and psychological trauma. In health terms, physical trauma may be a massive impact or a penetrating wound. The body goes into shock, and in the case of the latter it can be seen to be physically 'bleeding out'. Psychological trauma – the result of an upsetting event, can be even more challenging to overcome; it manifests with troubling emotions and anxiety. Trauma can leave people feeling numb, disconnected and unable to trust other people.

A PWQ of less than or equal to 1 indicates a traumatic culture.

Within the organization we see silos, with poor communication between teams. We see a lack of trust between team members. Traumatic cultures exhibit high levels of stress among staff, frequent errors and quality issues and an inability to manage day-to-day operations effectively. Blame becomes rife and, to deal with the high levels of stress, team members become numb and disconnected from their work. Companies often notice they are in a traumatic culture when they start running out of cash or losing staff in large numbers. They might have had an early warning if they were tracking their PWQ quarterly.

Case study: Apprenticeship training company

A change in funding rules by the UK Government was the external event that pushed an apprenticeship training company into trauma. Wholly reliant on government funding, paid as each learner was enrolled in an apprenticeship course, this dried up when the Government changed the rules at the end of a fiscal year. There were several months with no enrolments while the industry scrambled to adjust to the new working methods.

The organization was left with a backlog of hundreds of applications needing to be processed. It had been starved of cash for several weeks and was unable to start any new learners on their courses.

It did not have the financial reserves or a resilient culture in this situation, resulting in team members becoming stressed, mistakes being made, staff absences increasing and a blame culture erupting. Rather than being able to focus on processing the backlog of applications generated while there was a 'pause' on new starts, it found itself investing energy in dealing with internal issues that were counterproductive.

I guided them to focus on the number of applications completed on any given day, adopting a one-piece-flow strategy rather than a batch-processing approach.

> As a result, cash flow started to improve, while the team worked to improve internal operations and reorganize teams.

Like the body bleeds out with physical trauma, a company physically bleeds cash and people. For business owners or directors this leads to sleepless nights and a preoccupation with work, and it can severely impact relationships and life outside of work. Companies with a traumatic culture need to invest in self-care. The stress needs to be reduced, trust regained and anxieties diminished.

Gary Hamel believes that often organizations need to experience trauma before they improve:

> *'In most organizations changes comes in two flavours: trivial and traumatic. Review the history of the average organization, and you'll discover long periods of incremental fiddling punctuated by occasional bouts of frantic, crisis-driven change.'*[17]

Sadly, my experience supports this view. If organizations were to get in touch with me while they are living with a problematic culture and work to fix it, they would be more likely to weather any adverse events and avoid slipping into trauma.

A primary focus for traumatic organizations is cash flow. While focusing on fixing the trauma, the cash can be forgotten. When money or people flow out of a business,

[17] (Hamel 2009)

working capital frequently takes a knock. Focus here while you work to heal the trauma.

Case study: Distributor

A healthcare distribution client bought products from the Far East, stored them in its UK warehouse and then shipped them to wholesale customers as required. With lengthy shipping times between the Far East and the UK, it needed to plan four to six months in advance to ensure it had the right products on site to meet customer demand.

With thousands of pounds tied up in stock, cash flow was often a challenge, and managing the procurement was vital. The manual process for identifying products requiring reordering, a symptom of a problematic culture, eventually failed, causing several supply issues that needed to be sent via air freight rather than container ship. This cost significantly more and contributed to an acute cash flow issue for the business. It was this event, moving them from problematic to traumatic, that finally helped the business owner realize he could no longer rely on manual processes, which is when he engaged me to look at how productivity could be improved. In the meantime, he needed to focus on cash flow to keep things running. His approach to doing this was innovative, using his own credit card to pay a loan to the business, which in turn generated several days of cash flow to plug the gap – stressful and traumatic in equal measure.

Systematic

Systematic cultures represent a step-change in productivity. The dam of lethargy must be dismantled to allow ideas to flow freely. This culture is the first step to eliminating lethargy and embracing productivity and results from a conscious and thoughtful analysis of what is happening within a process or the entire business.

A PWQ of 1.7 to 2.5 indicates the range where an organization has started to work towards or has achieved a fully systematic culture. Systematic cultures will have a plan for understanding the business operations and arranging all aspects of the company so they are easily accessible and understood. Such activities might cause short-term pain to secure long-term gain.

Even the process of becoming systematic takes place systematically. Identifying critical business operations, prioritizing those ripe for improvement and then painstakingly reviewing all aspects of the relevant systems or processes in turn.

Information that was previously in silos flows freely in systematic organizations. When problems occur there is a systematic way of solving them, not only returning to the previous norm; it seeks to identify a new, higher standard and improves things for the future.

Tacit knowledge within the heads of the team members becomes explicit, written down and put together in a system of workflows that make what was previously confusing clear and what was once uncertain certain.

One way to think of a systematic business is to consider a chef who has been cooking for years and finally decides to publish a book of recipes. Even though they can prepare the dishes from memory, they must find a way to write the method down so others can do it. Systematic cultures can start leveraging people in ways problematic cultures cannot achieve.

Dusty Baker, an American former professional baseball player, sums this up nicely:[18]

> *'I love sharing my knowledge of hitting with others. Now coaches and players at all levels can learn my systematic approach to hitting a baseball with more consistency, mental strength and accuracy.'*[19]

Operating above the productivity line between lethargy and productivity, with cash flow and quality issues generally resolved, a systematic business focuses on capacity. Ensuring that the company extracts the maximum value from its available capacity is the key to long-term sustainability.

Case study: Audiovisual start-up

An entrepreneur-led audiovisual start-up needed help with a problematic culture. It had developed good expertise in its field and was attracting some

[18] (Wikipedia – Dusty Baker n.d.)

[19] (Collegiat Strength & Condidtioning Coaches Association (CSCCA) 2012)

high-end clients, yet it found that all too often things would go wrong with client projects and it would make little or no profit. The owner was frequently called upon to intervene and put things right, which made the organization heavily dependent upon him. With my support the owner systematically reviewed all aspects of the business operations, recognizing that a problematic culture was unsustainable for the organization's growth. He looked at many aspects of the business, from how work was priced, the internal systems his team members were using, how projects were run and the project management tools in use. Employee handbooks and internal policies were implemented, and recruitment for new team members became more formal and less of a gut feeling. Over a relatively short period he built a business operation that worked well even when he was not there, one that could cope with more and more projects successfully.

Many organizations I work with can show parts of their business that demonstrate systematic behaviours. Although, in numerical terms, an organization may find itself in the 'problematic' band, it may still have parts that fit the systematic description.

Typically, companies that sell physical products will have a systematic culture when managing the aspects involved in producing their products. They will have standardized catalogues or sales information to share with clients. The product will have a detailed specification or recipe listing the bill of materials and the production process. Tight quality assurance processes and benchmarks may exist; even the packaging can be described as systematic.

Sadly, in many such businesses, the surrounding organization may have been neglected, with the processes involved in taking orders, raising invoices, providing customer service, shipping, invoicing and dealing with returns being ignored.

Automatic

Automatic is *not* the same as 'on automatic'. The latter implies being operated or controlled without thought. We talk about being on 'automatic pilot' when we drive home from work – barely seeing the journey.

Automatic cultures are different from this. They are not cultures that exist in a stupor; quite the contrary, they have systematized everything in the business to operate automatically and habitually. To achieve this requires a tremendous amount of effort to be invested in understanding all the moving parts so that they can be automated. These cultures are highly proactive and highly productive.

Think about the automatic pilot in a plane. It has to understand wind speeds, cross-winds, weather conditions, direction, altitude and many other factors to fly the aircraft on behalf of the pilot. There is nothing 'passive' about creating something that can run automatically.

In these organizations we can expect a PWQ of 2.5 or more, indicating that the business is generating 2.5 times their salary in value for every person in the organization.

In automatic cultures the business and its people have developed productive habits. Habits are the human response to repeating something so often that it becomes part of who they are.

> *'Repetition of the same thought or physical action develops into a habit which, repeated frequently enough, becomes an automatic reflex.'*
>
> **Norman Vincent Peale**[20]

Automatic cultures have habits around troubleshooting, strategic planning, development and all the forward-looking processes crucial to a highly effective business. In automatic cultures, lethargy is rarely found anywhere. A healthy challenge of the status quo becomes habitual and automatic. Team members are characterized by having independent thought and being empowered to start, operate or move for the organization's good without constantly having to check in with someone else for authority or approval.

Just as an organization can be partially systematic, it may be partially automatic. It is common to find automated production lines where decision-making is done based on clearly documented algorithms and even by robots requiring no human decision-making.

Away from the factory floor, however, we increasingly see organizations automating aspects of their operations, from automated workflows that handle customer enquiries by presenting options for them to navigate, to customer journeys on websites that trigger follow-up emails based on

---

[20] (Peale 1989)

the visitor's behaviour and activities. To reach this level, all possible outcomes must be identified and the relevant logic must be put in place regarding how to deal with them.

Once an organization has been able to embed this culture in all its operations, providing team members with decision frameworks in which to operate, even when things do not go according to plan, we see genuinely automatic cultures. These organizations spend minimal time putting things right and most of their time delivering customer value.

To coin a phrase from Jim Collins, such organizations have fully understood their 'economic engine'.[21] Their challenge becomes how to ensure this engine is turning as fast as possible; how can they put as much throughput through the engine, knowing it will run without a hiccup?

Case study: Soft fruit packing

A soft fruit packing company interested in improving its productivity struggled to determine how it could deliver more value as it was already operating at a high level of productivity. It rarely experienced quality issues, waste or other common business problems. Team members packing the fruit benefitted from a well-laid-out warehouse, minimizing the handling journey and, consequently, time involved in the process.

The managing director needed help to see what else he could do to improve productivity. In this case

[21] (Collins, *How the Mighty Fall* 2009)

the answer lay in the focus word for this culture: throughput. The question we needed to ask was how he could increase throughput. He had two apparent options: the first was to expand the packing warehouse and the other was to operate multiple shifts. The latter represented the best way to increase productivity using the existing capital investment and was selected as the best route.

Overall culture

Using a combination of data and behavioural analysis, we can establish in which of the four productivity cultures an organization lies. We can even identify where an organization might have a Jekyll and Hyde personality, with one part falling within one culture, while the rest of the organization lies in another. Ultimately, the numerical value will provide the best indicator of the overall culture within an organization; in the same way as UK productivity growth is an average that encompasses the productive and the lethargic organizations, the PWQ informs an organization about which productivity culture prevails, despite differences between functions.

These cultures can be seen as different points on a continuum.

Figure 1 shows this continuum as an S-curve representing the PWQ. As we move from left to right across the graph, the x axis represents the effort being invested in productivity-generating activities. It shows how we move from one productivity culture to the next, starting with traumatic, through problematic, systematic and ultimately automatic. Using the S-curve highlights that the level of effort required to improve productivity is not linear and is often disproportionately high for relatively little gain at both ends of the curve.

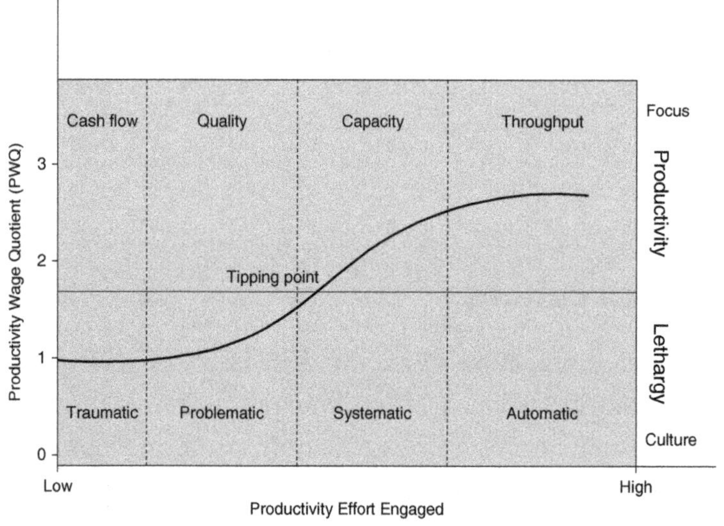

Figure 1 Productivity cultures

The tipping point, which has the potential to create upward momentum, is the move from problematic to systematic when the overriding culture switches from one characterized by lethargy to one characterized by productivity.

At the top of the chart we see the primary focus for each culture, namely cash flow, quality, capacity and throughput, which serves as a reminder of how to prioritize our activities.

Summary

So far, in Part 1 we have looked at the nature of productivity and the four distinct productivity cultures that drive organizations. In Part 2 – Improving Productivity, I set out the four levers that drive productivity. Part 3 – Finding Untapped Productivity outlines a methodology for identifying the pockets of untapped productivity within your organization. Finally, in Part 4 – Solutions, I look at how to identify your quick wins and big wins and ways in which you can start to put your ideas into practice so they will overcome lethargy and deliver the required productivity changes that you desire.

Part 2

Improving Productivity

Productivity Drivers

Now that we understand what productivity is, we can start to look at what drives productivity and, most importantly, if we can kick off the lethargy, where we might begin to focus our efforts. As we have already established, productivity measures labour output and value added. It can be calculated by taking net profit before tax and adding depreciation, wages and salaries to this figure. This number is then divided by the number of hours worked, or people (FTE).

$$\textit{Productivity} = \frac{\textit{wages and salaries} + (\textit{net profit} + \textit{depreciation})}{\textit{FTE}}$$

Let's look at each of these factors in turn and what drives them.

Wages and salaries

The *people* in your organization drive this number and it will increase as the number of people increase. Part of the value added created by your organization is spent on wages and salaries, therefore we can consider this figure to represent the value added created by your people in the equation above. How your team members behave will affect your wages and salaries bill; this makes *people* a key driver to consider.

FTE

The number of FTE roles in the organization is a measure of the effectiveness of the *process*. If we consider an organization where much of the work is carried out by robots on a factory floor, this number might be lower than one in which work is completed by hand throughout the factory. Being the fraction's denominator, the higher this number, the lower the overall result of the formula. Think of a pizza; if you cut it into two pieces (1/2), each piece is larger than if you cut it into quarters (1/4). Therefore, how you structure your processes and the tools used to operate them are significant factors in the overall productivity calculation.

One reason why economies are experiencing productivity challenges is that they have thrown people at their problems. The UK unemployment rate in February 2024 was 3.9%, one of the lowest rates for a decade, and the unemployment rate in the US at the end of 2023 was 3.6%, the lowest rate for decades.[22&23]

Net profit + depreciation

Net profit + depreciation is essentially net profit before depreciation. Several factors drive this number, so we need to separate out those that we have already considered and look at what is left. Therefore, we can ignore people and processes. An organization's net profit is partly driven by how it prices its products and services and the cost of producing or delivering them. For me, this is represented by the word *price*

[22] (Francis-Devine and Powell 2024)

[23] (Statista Research Department 2024)

and includes everything commercial regarding how products and services are bought and sold. Another significant factor in driving net profit is an organization's brand reputation, in other words, its *promise*.

If we take all of this, we can then rewrite the formula as follows:

$$\textit{Productivity} = \frac{\textit{People} + (\textit{Price} \times \textit{Promise})}{\textit{Process}}$$

The productivity pyramid

Together, people, promise, process and price form four sides of a pyramid.

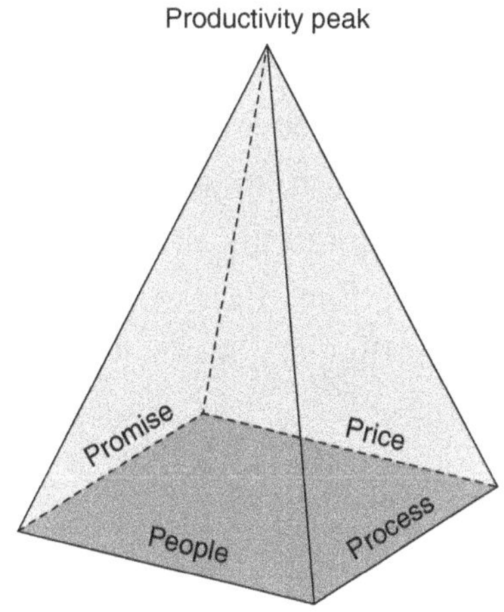

Figure 2 The productivity pyramid

To reach the productivity peak, all four areas require focus. It is challenging to get to the pinnacle, like climbing a pyramid, with its steep sides and smooth faces. Companies that cannot reach the peak on each side are left with a frustum rather than a pyramid, which sounds incredibly frustrating to me;

nevertheless, even if the peak is never reached, moving further up each side will yield incremental productivity gains.

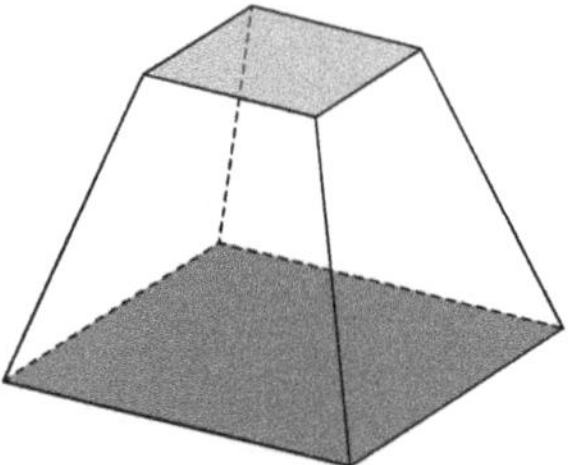

Figure 3 A fustrum

Companies with unequal efforts across the four areas are left with an irregular polyhedron that lacks a distinct name, as far as I can tell. If you know what it is called, I would love to hear!

To improve productivity, we must change at least one of these four elements. As with any fraction, the larger the number at the bottom, the smaller the result, so it stands to reason that at the very least we need to increase the top of the fraction without increasing the bottom, or reduce the number at the bottom while maintaining the number at the top. Ideally we need to increase the number at the top *and* reduce the number at the bottom.

There are many ways to achieve this, so to start with let's examine each of the four elements in turn to better understand them.

Promise

In order to 'trick' the brain to overcome this lethargy, we need to engage emotions. To create an impetus for action, we need purpose, connection, agency, autonomy and an opportunity for creativity and involvement or stake in our work. One way to do this is to revisit our organization's promise.

Promise is my word for what has been referred to by many other authors as 'value proposition'. It is the promise an organization makes to its customers when they are transacting with it. Promise contributes to productivity because not only does it help provide purpose, connection and autonomy within the team, but an organization that delivers upon a clearly defined promise is more likely to maintain sufficient demand for its products and services to use all of its capacity. Organizations that are not clear on their promise or fail to deliver on it can find themselves with extra capacity they cannot sell. An organization's promise is so important that it is worth considering whether it needs to be insured. If there are high levels of risk associated with your promise, and keeping it might result in significant financial cost, underwriting the ability to keep that promise could be astute.

Case study: Crystal Ski

Crystal Ski offers customers a snow promise. If there is no snow, they will do everything they can to get customers on the slopes, with the option to change holiday dates in the four days before travelling if there is insufficient skiing in the resort.[24] While on the surface this promise may help them fill their capacity, it is a promise they cannot control, one that can backfire. In December 2022, when the snow came very late, customers travelling to Bulgaria were faced with no snow. In order to honour its promise, Crystal contacted its customers in the week prior to departure to explain that, although they could travel, Crystal could not offer any skiing. In the face of this dilemma, most customers took the option to rebook later in the season. This left Crystal with empty flights and beds – surplus capacity they still had to pay for. With a promise intrinsically linked to the unpredictable weather, I have to hope they had insurance in place.

An organization's promise is not about what they sell, it is about working out what they give. This is articulated succinctly in a quote attributed to Charles Revson, founder of Revlon:

[24] (Crystal Ski 2023/24)

> *'In the factory we make cosmetics, in the store we sell hope.'*

The key for an organization is to understand its promise and to ensure that all its team members know what it is. When they do, if they behave in line with the promise, team members will share it with the market. It is this that builds brand value, which, when a business is sold for more than the assets in its balance sheet, is valued as 'goodwill'.

The marketing philosophy and system outlined in *The Brand Bucket®* defines a brand as:

> *'Every action that affects the relationship between an organization and its consumer.'*[25]

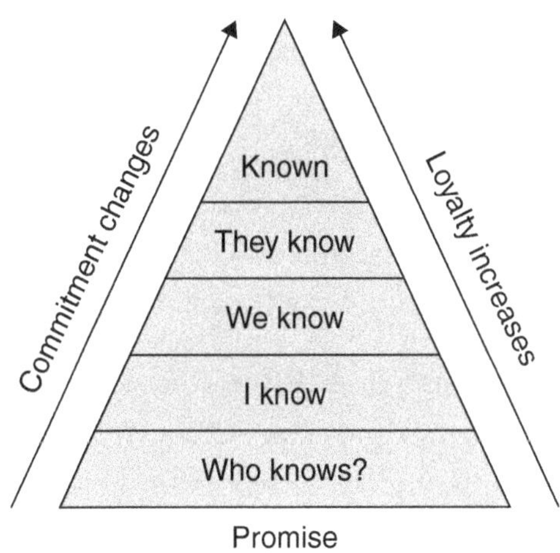

Figure 4 Promise side of the productivity pyramid

When we understand this, we can see how promise impacts all the other three productivity levers. Suppose every action affects how our customers interpret and validate our ability to

---

[25] (Wynter, *The Brand Bucket: Make Your Marketing Work* 2010)

keep our promise. In that case, it is intrinsically linked with our processes (how we deliver), our people (the relationships we build) and the price (how we price what we sell and what we pay team members and suppliers).

Organizations can move up the productivity pyramid by moving themselves further up the ladder on the promise side of the pyramid. Let's look at each level in turn.

Level 1: Who knows?

The first level of promise is a situation where it is no longer clear within an organization what the promise was or should be. This can happen over time when an organization loses its way. When forming an organization, most founders clearly know the promise they represent. However, over time, this can be lost. The promise that worked 10, 20, 50 or more years ago may no longer be relevant. The situation is like having a worn-out cog that has lost its teeth over time and become a smooth circle. Even though it may be a helpful part, it can no longer serve the function for which it was initially designed.

An outdated promise is as bad as one where nobody seems to know the original promise. This can happen when the founder moves on, and those who buy the organization may not understand or believe in the original promise. This can often occur where the original promise is based on function and technology rather than benefits and emotional connection.

Case study: Kodak

Kodak is an example of an organization that needed to adjust its promise in the face of new technology and a changing landscape. The company sold reasonably priced cameras and made its profits mainly by selling the film and processing services that followed, in much the same way ink-jet manufacturers sell printers and the inks they use today. Kodak was aware of the digital revolution; in fact, one of its engineers invented the first digital camera. Despite investing in digital technology, it underestimated its competitors who developed superior products, and management was concerned that digital would cannibalize its traditional film sales. Its failure came from focusing on products rather than the value it provided. Rather than asking, 'What business are we in?' it asked, 'How do we sell more products?' It was so hung up that it failed to adapt and lead change, and by the time it did there were already multiple new entrants into the market.

Level 2: I know

'I know' may occur with founder owners who have built an organization with an explicit promise and have failed to communicate this to everyone else. They may have focused their training and onboarding on the process aspects rather than sharing the why (i.e. the promise) with new team members.

Alternatively, managers who have lost touch with the promise fail to share it with the new team members they recruit. So, we end up with a situation where the only person who remembers the promise and is trying to ensure that it is delivered is the person at the top.

The founder can find this incredibly frustrating when an organization is stuck at I know. Suppose none of the team knows why the business exists. In that case, the decision-making process is detached from the company's core promise and purpose, resulting in decisions that do not fit with the organization.

Case study: Clothing manufacturer

When I ran a software development company, one of our clients sold clothing. In the same way that Revlon made lipstick and sold hope, this client was run by a founder who knew he was in the image business. When I visited, I received tea served in a very particular way. A round pewter tray was laid with a fringed napkin. The tea, made with cardamom pods, was served in a pot and kept warm by a cashmere knitted cosy; the coffee was kept warm by a cashmere knitted jacket on the cafetiere. We drank out of handle-less glasses; if you wanted sugar, it was a rough cube of brown sugar.

The responsibility for serving drinks to guests lay with the office assistant, and the person in this role changed on a frighteningly regular basis. Over the years I worked with this client, the tea service appeared to lose its way. This was an example of how the organization was led by a founder who knew they were in the image business but, due to high staff turnover, many of the staff believed they were in the clothing business.

When an organization is at I know, not only do the wider team members not fully understand the organization's promise, neither do its customers. A confused offering makes for a confusing position in the marketplace. Rather, like who knows?, customers may receive inconsistent service or experience, never knowing what to expect.

Level 3: We know

At 'we know', an organization is aligned on its promise, and all team members know what they are about. Most of us have heard the apocryphal story that illustrates this vividly. It is reported that in 1962, during a visit to NASA, President Kennedy spotted a janitor carrying a broom. He interrupted his visit to ask the janitor what he was doing. The janitor apparently responded, 'I'm putting a man on the moon, Mr President.'

This is an excellent demonstration of how an organization can benefit when everyone knows the promise. The janitor was part of the 1962 NASA space team. We can think of lots of examples of similar stories.

Case study: GB rowing team

The GB men's eight rowing team set themselves the goal in 1998 of achieving gold at the 2000 Sydney Olympics, despite being an underachieving team. They created a promise that all team members knew; they would win gold at the Olympics, and they would achieve this by judging every decision based on whether it would help the boat go faster. On 25 September 2000, the team won gold, proving what is possible when all team members are aligned behind a single promise.

Since then, team member Ben Hunt-Davis has gone on to extrapolate the principles they followed in the book *Will it Make the Boat Go Faster?*[26]

However, the external market and customers may not fully understand the promise at the we know level. In the examples above, it was okay that the promise was an internal alignment promise, as neither organization was a commercial entity seeking to sell its products and services to customers. In the case of the GB men's eight rowing team, one could even argue that it might have been a closely guarded secret

[26] (Hunt-Davis and Beveridge 2011)

before the Sydney Olympics. However, for most commercial organizations, being the best-kept secret is not desirable, nor likely to help increase overall productivity.

The challenge for we know organizations is to find ways to communicate what they are about with their customers and potential customers. We often see enterprising organizations that have built a great business, delivering their promise day in and day out to a loyal customer base. However, they have struggled to expand to reach their full potential because their ability to communicate this promise is hampered in some way.

Level 4: They know

'They know' is a realistic ambition for most organizations. The internal team members and existing and potential customers understand the organization's promise. These organizations have worked to encapsulate the promise throughout their operations and marketing and sales communications to ensure there is no ambiguity about the promise.

There will be plenty of local they know examples in your area.

Case study: Motor garage

We have a local motor garage that is always completely booked out. The owner has set himself up to provide motorbike MOTs to the local area. It is known locally that if you want a quick MOT, you can book in at 8:30, and it will be done first thing, and then you are off on your way. If you are not in a rush, you can drop off your bike first thing and then pop back later in the day when he calls to let you know it is complete. He gets so busy that he has had to enlist the help of his wife to handle bookings and invoicing, and he is so good at what he does that the bike owners also bring him their cars for MOTs and repairs. He has filled his capacity, he is clear about what he does, and everyone knows this. He promises to do everything in his power to keep you on the road, even if that means he works late nights and weekends. One could argue that he is a victim of his own success.

Many organizations aspire to be the 'next best thing', to 'go viral' or to have some level of notoriety that can boost their fame. In reality, most organizations only need to be known in a relatively small geographical area; they know does not have to mean you are a household name.

Level 5: Known

The highest level on the promise ladder is 'known'. This is when the organization has become a household name beyond a small geography, where the organization and the wider world know the promise. That might be within an industry, a region, nationally or even internationally. If we think of major brands, there will be few people who have not heard of and do not know the promise behind some of the world's most well-known organizations. For example:

- Google
- Apple
- Nike
- NATO
- Red Cross

Organizations that benefit from being known find themselves in an envious position where they can easily generate interest for their products and services. The annual Wimbledon tennis tournament operates a ballot due to the popularity of tickets. It is massively oversubscribed, particularly within its market of tennis fans. Other examples include the queues outside Apple stores upon the release of new products.

Known brands can leverage existing customers when they launch new products and services.

Case study: Dyson

When British manufacturer Dyson, well known for its revolutionary vacuum cleaners, announced its intention to enter the haircare market, many doubted its decision. However, when it launched the Dyson Supersonic in 2016, it received rave reviews and became an instant success despite its hefty price tag.[27]

[27] (Shacknai 2022)

However, being known does not mean you must be an internationally famous organization. It does mean that you need to be known within your own marketplace. It might be that you are known in your particular industry, and even if they do not buy from you, most of your target customers and suppliers would know of you and what you stand for.

To be known within our productivity context (i.e. at the top of the pyramid), an organization needs to be known for what it stands for.

Of course, the reality is that some organizations become known for the wrong things. When this occurs there is a conflict between what customers understand as the promise, based on what they have previously been told, and what they now understand to be true. When this happens, we can describe the organization as falling dramatically to who knows? The scale of being a household name, combined with the result of revealing a significant break in the widely accepted promise can have dramatic adverse consequences. History is peppered with examples of this.

Case study: Ratners jewellers

In April 1991, at a conference of the Institute of Directors, Gerald Ratner of Ratners, a popular British chain of jewellery stores, described the products as 'total crap'.[28] The result of this comment was that

[28] (Davis 1993)

customers stayed away from the stores and the value of the group dropped by some £500 million as shares dropped from £4 to 7p.[29]

Case study: Amazon

Amazon is an organization whose promise is centred around customer service. It aims to provide the best customer service. However, its reputation for setting up its operations in such a way that it avoids paying corporation tax in many countries means that some people and businesses have decided to boycott it. This is an example of Amazon being known, and not for the reasons it would prefer. In some areas the negative reputation has outweighed the deliberate promise it has chosen to make.

The effect of brand loyalty

As we climb the promise triangle, we see a marked increase in loyalty and commitment. This loyalty may take the form of both customer and brand loyalty.

Brand loyalty represents a long-term commitment from customers to make repeat purchases from a brand. Consequently, it represents a significant driver in an

[29] (Ratner 2007)

organization's ability to drive profitability. Brand-loyal customers believe that purchases from their chosen brand are superior to those of their competitors, or they may have developed an emotional connection with the brand.

On the other hand, customer loyalty is based on factors such as pricing, rewards programmes and discounts, and is fuelled by benefits and incentives. As such, brand loyalty is more valuable than customer loyalty.

Why is loyalty important? We should remember that productivity is a financial metric, and one of the constituent parts is net profits. In that case, these are partially driven by an organization's ability to build loyal customers who will make repeat purchases.

In 1990, a study reported in the *Harvard Business Review* found that

> *'in industry after industry... increasing customer retention rates by 5% increase profits by 25% to 95%.'*[30]

This is due to the relatively high cost of acquiring new customers, which can make them unprofitable in the early years. Over time, if these customers remain loyal, the cost of serving them reduces and, as the volume of purchases rises, the relationships start to deliver more significant returns.

A more recent 2020 study reported in the *Harvard Business Review* repeated the methodology in several e-commerce sectors and found that not only did the same loyalty economics work, they were also exaggerated on the internet.[31] The cost

---

[30] (Sasser, Jr. and Reichheld 1990)

[31] (Reichheld and Schefter 2000)

of acquiring a new web customer can be higher than in a traditional retail channel; however, the study found that web customers became fiercely loyal to their preferred brands, with visiting the supplier's sites becoming part of their daily routine.

In 2018, InMoment found that 61% of customers will go out of their way to buy from the brands to which they are loyal.[32] In 2020, Zendesk found this figure to be 52%.[33] The InMoment study also found that 77% of customers have stayed loyal to the same brands for at least ten years. Meanwhile, PwC found that loyal customers are willing to forgive the odd mistake, and 83% of US customers would not stop interacting with a brand they love after one bad experience.[34]

The figures are clear: increasing customer and brand loyalty increases profitability.

Who knows?

When an organization operates at who knows?, the effort to acquire new customers is significant. As a little-known organization with no clear market promise, the promise is built on a transaction-by-transaction basis with the associated costs that entails. If the value of each sale is significant enough, it may still be possible to be profitable at this stage; however, for the vast majority of organizations, this personal hand-holding through the sales process will come at a cost

---

[32] (InMoment 2018)
[33] (Zendesk 2020)
[34] (PwC 2018)

that is unlikely to be justified. There is little commitment from customers; they may well purchase once and then go elsewhere at this stage. If they do purchase more than once and receive different experiences, that may reduce loyalty and commitment as they are prompted to shop around for a more consistent service. Marketing departments can help to raise an organization's profile so that when they are approached, potential customers are familiar with the name, even if they do not know what it does.

I know

At I know, an individual may drive loyalty; for example, the founder or owner of an organization. Loyalty can be tied to that person, and should they leave or move, the customers may transfer with them. Commitment and loyalty are at the level of an individual. We can all think of examples where the customer relationship is with an individual. When they move, the customers go with them – hairdressers, for example, or salespeople who move to a competitor. To retain customers when an individual leaves, there needs to be something beyond the individual, creating commitment and loyalty from customers. Where brand loyalty exists here, it is based on the connection with the individual rather than the brand as a whole, and is therefore vulnerable to changes in personnel.

We know

By the time we have moved up to we know, we can see a group of team members providing consistent customer experiences aligned to a central brand promise. Relationships will be less dependent upon individuals and will be more team-based. The organization may have generated customer loyalty and the team may be committed to the organization. Brand loyalty is not yet well established.

They know

When they (customers) know, like and trust an organization's promise, we start to see an increase in repeat purchases and the beginning of loyal customers, developing brand loyalty and generating referrals. Referrals are often the lowest-cost method of acquiring customers, so having a customer base that is sufficiently loyal that it will recommend you to their friends is a significant benefit to any organization. In 2018 InMoment found that 75% of loyal customers will recommend a brand to friends and family.[35]

Known

By the time we have reached known, the organization has created brand loyalty and significant commitment from within its customers. For example, we only need to look to organizations such as Apple, where customers will stand in queues for hours, even overnight, to get their hands on a new iPhone when it is launched. Although it may not have always been the case, these days Apple's 'implicit promise' is to create a smooth experience as long as you are within Apple's ecosystem.[36] Although arguably more expensive than alternatives and with no discernible technical differences (in

35 (InMoment 2018)

36 (de Ternay 2024)

isolation), iPhones consistently sell quickly, with customers often evangelical about the products.

Price

Price plays a vital role in an organization's productivity. It is an element often overlooked as we get tied up trying to be more efficient or effective and forget that productivity is a financial metric.

Within this model, price represents everything connected with the commercials around how an organization buys, makes and sells its products or services.

At the most superficial level, if we increase our prices, sell the same volume and nothing else changes, our productivity will appear to increase. This, of course, is not the case. It is a bit like saying that a bartender in London who serves 15 pints @ £3.00 each is more productive than a bartender in the north of the country who serves 15 pints at the same time @ £2.50 each. They are both as productive individually; however, the whole system is not as productive because the total value created (assuming both bar tenders are paid the same) will be higher in London.[37]

Nevertheless, understanding this effect on productivity helps us understand the role price plays in generating increased

---

[37] (Martin-Fagg n.d.)

productivity. At a base level, it demonstrates the need for a pricing strategy and not to leave pricing to chance.

Have a pricing strategy

Not having a pricing strategy is like going to war without a plan. At the very least we need to know why we charge what we charge for our products or services. What is the basis of our calculation, and is it sound? Often, companies do not fully understand the true cost of what they sell and include things they should not or miss things out when calculating this. What do our prices say about us? We can all think of examples of what is essentially the same product being priced very differently and how, if the price is too low, we perceive it to be lower value. Some brands set out to be the lowest-cost varieties, while others aim to be at the top end of the scale.

Then there is the price we need to charge. This price covers our costs and generates a realistic profit margin for the organization. Sometimes the market sets a value for a given product or service and, unless we can differentiate ourselves significantly, it is difficult to charge any more. Considering all this, we can establish the price we should charge for a given product or service.

All too often I come across prices set across the board using the same algorithm, irrespective of what they are or who they are targeted at. Some products within a company's portfolio could likely command a higher value than others. Yet, cost-plus pricing policies generate a uniform sales price without considering the market.

As with our other productivity levers, there are five pricing levels, each generating potentially more significant productivity gains.

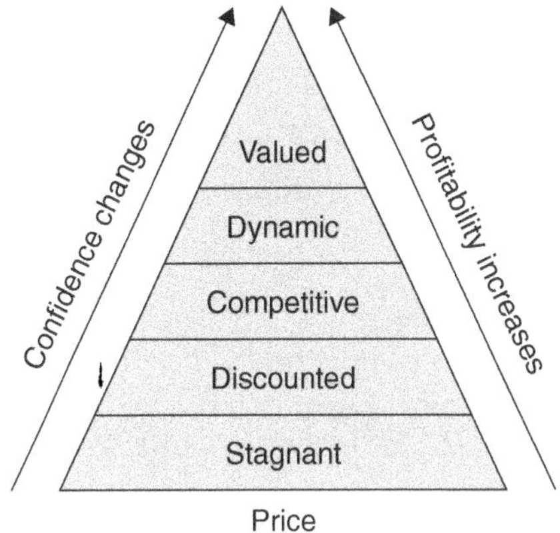

Figure 5 Price side of the productivity pyramid

Knowing your break-even point

It may sound obvious, but it is nevertheless worth stating that understanding your break-even point (BEP) is crucial to setting a pricing strategy. The BEP is the point at which your profit (value added) from sales equals your overheads. Unless you generate more than your BEP, you will be making a loss, even if you charge a lot for a service.

This is not always a simple calculation because different products and services will have different BEPs. Customers can have different BEPs when considering the total cost of looking after a customer.

Where possible, overheads should not be apportioned to individual products or services. Any way of doing this takes time and is almost always subjective. We need to add up all of our overheads to calculate a BEP. This is the figure on one side of the equation and is usually expressed as a figure for a year, a quarter or a month.

The number on the other side of the equation is the profit from sales (value added) for each product or service multiplied by the number of units of that product or service you sell in the same period (i.e. a year, a quarter or a month).

For example:

number of units sold x value added per sale = total overheads

Calculating the BEP for any given unit is then a process of working out either the value added you need to generate from each product or service to make the equation balance or the quantity of the product or service you need to sell at the current value added to make the equation balance.

$$\textit{break-even value added} = \frac{\textit{total overheads}}{\textit{number of units sold}}$$

Understand your true overhead

Overheads are the things you pay for, whether or not you sell something. In many organizations the profit of a product includes an element of overheads. This can be unhelpful when establishing a pricing strategy because overheads stay the same despite the level of sales.

The crucial rule when considering whether a cost is an overhead is whether it behaves like an overhead. The question is: if we had a short period of sales downturn, would I be able to eliminate this cost? If the answer is no, the cost is an overhead. As the saying goes, 'If it walks like a duck, quacks like a duck and swims like a duck, it is likely to be a duck.'

Many organizations that sell time include the cost (salary and benefits) of that time in the variable expenses that are used to calculate the costs of sale. However, this is misleading, as were there to be a lull in sales, it is unlikely that those staff would immediately be let go. They are, in fact, overheads. In other industries, an element of overhead allocation is apportioned to products as part of their costs; for example, the cost of a factory, which again is misleading because, if sales drop, the costs of running the building rarely drop in a directly proportionate way.

My suggestion is to treat these costs as overheads rather than as part of your product costs, which may differ from how your organization currently reports its financials. If you experience resistance to such a change, consider how you might structure your reporting by adding an interim sub-total of value added before gross profit until everyone is confident of its benefits. It is also worth noting that management accounts can be presented differently from the statutory financial accounts, with which all companies are obliged to comply. It is, therefore, possible to include more traditional 'overhead' costs in the financial accounts, while adopting a 'true overhead' approach for management accounting.

Level 1: Stagnant

When I ran a software development company many years ago, we made the mistake of maintaining our consultancy rate for several consecutive years. This is known as 'stagnant' pricing. The word stagnant describes something that is characterized by a lack of development, advancement or progressive movement. We should have increased prices annually by at least a small amount, ideally in line with inflation. However, having not done this, we faced the unenviable situation where we needed to go to clients with a significant price hike all in one go or face financial consequences.

A good indicator of how prices need to increase to stay in line with inflation is to look at the Retail Price Index data and understand the difference between the index on the date you last updated your prices and today. This will help you understand the increase in retail prices, aka inflation. For example, in the UK, £1 in December 2010 had increased to £1.64 by the end of 2019.

It is all too easy to fall into the trap of stagnant pricing. A competitive market can make it difficult to increase prices, especially at times when the cost of many commodities is falling rather than growing. It is far easier to justify price increases when everyone is experiencing increasing supply chain prices.

When you are trapped with stagnant pricing, getting back on track can feel like a big jump. It can feel like you are on a boat moving away from the jetty, and as the boat drifts further and further away, it is too scary to make the jump. Stagnant pricing is often the result of a lack of price confidence, which then compounds the challenge of making the jump.

If you realize your pricing is stagnant, one option is to implement a series of regular price increases more frequently than annually to get you back on track. The other is to hold conversations with customers or clients to discuss why prices are jumping so much.

A critical tool that can help with this is the price increase matrix. A copy of this can be downloaded from my website at https://resources.amandasokell.com. This matrix helps to understand the impact of a price increase on the value added you can charge. For example, if your value-added margin is x% and you raise your prices by y%, you can afford to lose z% of your sales/customers and still make the same value added. This tool can reassure team members and colleagues that the proposed price increases will have the desired effect.

Level 2: Discounted

Many companies I have worked with have a default policy of discounting their products and services. It is almost as if the price list does not exist, and each customer is charged what the salesperson thinks they will pay by offering a discount. The issue is that default discounting is a race to the bottom, turning your product or service into a commodity.

Default discounting takes many forms. It can be a specially negotiated price for each customer or a standard x% discount on every proposal, and rarely is it part of a pricing strategy. Discounting in this way means that all our customers buy at a 'sale' price, and we have no customers who pay what someone worked out our products or services were worth.

Rather than routinely offering discounts, they should be something requested. Whenever we agree on a discount, we are devaluing what we offer, and to avoid this a discount needs to be a trade-off. For example, a discount for early payment or a discount in return for a testimonial or a referral to another customer. Discounts can, however, be used strategically to significant effect when selling surplus or time-limited stock or using up spare capacity that would otherwise go to waste.

Of course, some discounts are not genuine; they are only for perception. Some organizations are known to set their price list artificially high and then offer discounts from this. I call this a phantom price list. A recent *Which?* report highlighted that many of the so-called 'Black Friday' deals that appear at the end of November are no better value than the same products a few weeks earlier, mainly because the prices were raised artificially a few weeks before the Black Friday sale.[38] While this might work in some industries, as a practice it can backfire. I am sure we can all think of examples, like the double-glazing salespeople who come into your home, quote several thousand pounds to replace your windows and then, after making a phone call, offer you the same windows for a significantly lower price.

Level 3: Competitive

Many organizations find themselves in the world of competitive tendering or pricing. This is where they submit tenders, proposals or quotes for products and services, knowing they will be competing against others in the market. As a result, they price their product or services in line and

---

[38] (Which? 2023)

possibly lower than they expect their competitors to do. This type of pricing is all about benchmarking within the marketplace; again, the effect is to commoditize the product or service. If nothing separates your product or service from your competitors, price becomes the only determining factor.

Before it closed in 2020, the website MySupermarket allowed consumers to compare the price of groceries across different supermarkets. Having price-checked it across local supermarkets, it even provided a facility to split the order and place it with two or three providers, thereby getting the best prices for each and every product. In this way, saving several pounds a week in a weekly shop was possible.

The problem with this for supermarkets is that they need customers to buy a full range of goods from them, some of which they make a low margin on and others where the margin is higher. When customers only purchase low-margin goods or those on special offer, the supermarket can lose money overall.

If your organization is stuck with 'competitive' pricing, read more about dynamic pricing to see how you can break free.

Level 4: Dynamic

With 'dynamic' pricing, prices are not all the same. The same product or service might sell at a different price depending on the customer, the timing, the urgency, or several other factors. An excellent example of this is airline flights, which increase in cost the closer you get to the flight date. Hairdressers often offer pensioners a lower-priced haircut on a weekday when they might otherwise be quiet, and charge more for wedding hair during peak Saturday slots.

To use dynamic pricing effectively, a good starting point is understanding an organization's capacity correctly. Capacity is how many of a given product or service can be generated within a period of time. For example, companies selling time may have a defined number of hours in a month that they expect to be available for billing. A production line can generally produce a fixed quantity of products (without running overtime or additional shifts). All companies will have a constraint on the number of products or services they can sell, and working this out is an essential step towards dynamic pricing.

Bob Gorton calls this a 'critical resource limitation' (CRL) in his book *Boosting Sales: Increasing Profits Without Breaking the Bank*.[39] This builds upon the concept of 'productive hours' outlined by Brian Warnes in *The Genghis Khan Guide to Business*.[40] If you sell hours, your critical resource capacity is the number of productive hours rather than the number of hours for which employees are paid; he notes that, generally, only 1,000 hours out of 1,400 are 'productive'. An excellent way to determine the constraint for your organization is to consider that if your sales were to suddenly double, which resource required to deliver your product or service would be the hardest to increase quickly.

Once you know your capacity and have already calculated your total overheads, you can start to look at the amount

39 (Gorton 2007)

40 (Warnes 1984)

of overhead that each unit of your capacity needs to cover to break even. This is a different type of break-even point, known as the CRL break-even point. It might be expressed as £x/hour, £x/machine hour or £x/customer.

$$\textit{CRL break-even point} = \frac{\textit{total overheads}}{\textit{quantity of the CRL}}$$

This BEP is a crucial factor in the use of dynamic pricing. While it is possible to sell below this point, this needs to be reserved for strategic purposes. It might be used to sell surplus capacity (once all other targets have been met), it could be used to provide a sweetener for a new client (once all other targets have been met), and occasionally it might be the result of an order or project that has gone wrong.

To use dynamic pricing to its best effect, the organization then builds a pricing model that allows for a proportion of its total capacity to be sold at different price points. For example, because life never runs perfectly, 10% of the capacity may be sold for less than the BEP, and a further 20% might be sold between BEP and the ideal selling price to achieve our target profit, then let's say 40% needs to be sold at a point 20% higher than the BEP to deliver a healthy profit, while the final 30% might be sold at a point that is 25% or higher than the BEP. By creating price bands that generate different levels of value added, team members can flex prices within the framework to generate the most value added possible. The highest prices would be charged to the client who wants something urgently or where there is the opportunity to add value to the services in other ways.

Dynamic pricing based on the value added per unit of CRL allows an entire organization to align behind a single metric. Understanding the CRL and pricing everything based on this can help all parts of an organization understand their role in achieving the organization's objectives. Using this model, there are only three levers that team members need to factor into their actions: one is the revenue generated (i.e. the price paid by the customer), the second is the (true) costs incurred to provide the service or make the product, and the last is how the CRL is utilized. Often, understanding this concept can fix several underlying issues within an organization.

Case study: Whisky industry

Old St Andrews Whisky used dynamic pricing and the concept of the CRL to good effect when it realized that its limited supply of 55,000 litres of whisky could be sold in one-litre bottles or 100cl miniatures. The gross margin percentage was similar, as the cost of the bottles was essentially the same. However, the value added per litre was very different. It could either sell 55,000 litres in one-litre bottles @ £1.00 of value added per litre, or 55,000 litres in 100cl bottles @ £15.00 of value added per litre. The latter provided a total added value of £825,000 rather than £55,000. Understanding this completely changed the pricing strategy and, ultimately, the company's business strategy. Doing this moved the company from making a loss to creating a healthy profit.

Level 5: Valued

A 'valued' pricing strategy is one where an organization has researched and knows how its customers love its goods and services. Value is what customers receive relative to the price they pay, and clients use four elements in determining value, which is only partially affected by the price charged.

Value is also affected by the invisible cost of doing business and the quality of the products and services; that is, the customer's entire experience.

We can express customer value as a formula as follows:

$$\text{Customer Value} = \frac{(\text{Product Quality} + \text{Service Quality})}{(\text{Price} + \text{Cost of Doing Business})}$$

This customer value equation above is the central model of the service profit chain, presented by Heskett, Sasser and Schlesinger in their 1997 book *The Service Profit Chain*.[41]

We can all recall low-cost services that are also low in value.

Case study: Contrasting flight experiences

I once found myself on a flight to Aarhus in Denmark late at night. I should have been on a flight to Malmö in Sweden for a city break; however, having missed the check-in, the only way to resurrect the weekend was

[41] (Heskett , Sasser Jr. and Schlesinger 1997)

to take the last flight to the region, which happened to be Aarhus, and then travel by train to Malmö. At the point of booking the flight, in my hurried desperation I did not think to check where Aarhus airport lies, relative to the city centre. This was back at the turn of the century, before the smartphone became ubiquitous. Upon arrival, I discovered that it was nearly 50km to Aarhus, with few hotel options nearby, and as the flight landed so late at night there was no public transport available. It was one of the consequences of booking a very low-cost fare.

Contrast this to the service received when I travelled to Los Angeles in the early 2000s on business. I was booked to fly Virgin Upper Class, and in those days the ticket included a complimentary limo service, where a limo arrives at your house to collect you and take you to the airport, and another one picks you up at your landing airport and takes you to your final destination at the other end.

Different people value different things; a busy executive will value the upper-class service and be happy to pay extra for the smooth, hassle-free transit, while a backpacker is unlikely to be willing to pay the extra money for such a service because their priorities are different.

A valued pricing strategy prices goods and services in terms of their value to the customer without being constrained by what they cost to produce. It is the antithesis of a cost-plus pricing strategy, where the cost of a product or service is calculated, and then a markup is added. With valued pricing, the markup could be a few pounds or many thousands – the focus is on what it is worth to the customer rather than what it costs to make. One of the factors to consider when moving towards a pricing model of this nature is how you can increase the value to your customer, providing you with the ability to charge more without causing a significant increase in your costs.

Apple is an excellent example of valued pricing. Most will agree that the hardware differences between two comparable products, one Apple and another (e.g. Windows PC, Samsung Phone, etc.), are marginal. If anything, Apple's hardware technology may be inferior. However, Apple has created significant value in how it packages its products, how they all work together, how they have made them easy to use, and through its after-sales care via Genius bars and stores. As a result, they can command significantly higher prices than their alternatives despite not being especially technically superior.

Case study: Marketing workshops

A marketing consultant I know used a novel strategy to work out the value of his workshops. He ran two-day residential marketing workshops for business owners in small groups of up to eight people. He increased the fee by £500 each time he ran the workshop. Over a few months, he tripled the price of the seminars and could still fill the seats. The eventual price being charged bore no relationship to the costs of putting on the workshops, which included the hotel accommodation and meals, some printing and his and his assistant's time.

Case study: Patent lawyer

A former client shared a story about a patent lawyer they knew who struggled with too much work and decided to reduce her client base. She would increase her prices, expecting some of her clients not to be prepared to pay the higher rates, so her workload would drop. She contacted them all and explained she was doubling her rates. However, what happened was different from what she predicted. All her clients continued to work with her, and she became even busier. Clients valued that she was in demand and were prepared to pay a premium for someone so popular.

Case study: Knowing where to tap

There is a famous business parable that may have been derived from an original published in 1908.[42] Today there are many versions of the parable that have a similar theme. A business owner is faced with a crucial faulty machine. They ask many experts if they can fix the machine, and none is able to do so. Eventually an elderly engineer is called in to see if they can help. The engineer spends some time looking at the machine and, relatively quickly, retrieves a hammer and taps the machine, kick-starting it into life. When the engineer renders the bill, it is far higher than the business owner expects, given the time the engineer has spent fixing the problem. The business owner challenges this and asks for a breakdown. The response varies based on the currency and the date of the parable's telling. The original was set in the UK in a pre-decimal era of pounds, shillings and pence. The bill was broken down as follows:

For tapping the machine	£0.10s
For knowing where to tap	£10.00
Total	£10.10s

The moral of the story is that the knowledge gained through years of experience has value beyond the time taken to execute

42 (Society of Estate Clerks of Works 1908)

a task. In this case, the engineer valued their experience at 20 times the time involved in tapping the machine.[43]

Go the extra mile

The concept of going the extra mile is not new. Napoleon Hill wrote about it in his book *Think and Grow Rich*, first published in 1937.[44]

> *'You can start right where you stand and apply the habit of going the extra mile by rendering more service and better service than you are now being paid for.'*

This excerpt from a later edition explains his thinking here:

> *'Before you even start to negotiate for a readjustment of your salary in your present position, or to seek employment elsewhere, be sure that you are worth more than you now receive. It is one thing to want money – everyone wants more – but it is something entirely different to be worth more! Many people mistake their wants for their just dues. Your financial requirements or wants have nothing whatever to do with your worth. Your value is established entirely by your ability to render useful service or your capacity to induce others to render such service.'*

When we consider valued pricing, this concept of going the extra mile is about helping to understand what customers value. Once this is understood, it can be incorporated into your services, and you can therefore charge for it. The challenge is to keep looking for ways to add value and go the

---

43 (£1 = 20 shillings 1908)

44 (Hill 1939)

extra mile to justify increases in price. Ultimately, whatever you add in as your 'extra mile' needs to provide value for the customer.

My good friend and marketing practitioner Barnaby Wynter encourages his clients to think about what they can 'give away' when customers contract with them.[45] He keeps asking, 'And what else?' until they really feel they cannot give away anything else. It is interesting to see how much gets 'added in' as value before it starts to hurt.

I would take it one stage further, however. I see the 'and what else?' exercise as a creative one that helps to identify value-added products and services we might previously not have considered. If we consider the Apple example, the premium price is achieved due to the extra services surrounding the physical product. Once we have this list, I would use this to inform the right price point for the offering, which may be more than when you originally started thinking about what you can 'give away'.

Price confidence

Price confidence is described as a concept contributing to price satisfaction by consumers.[46]

> *'Price confidence addresses the question to what extent the consumer believes that an offered price is currently favourable. (Dillar 1997/2000)'*

---

[45] (Wynter, The Brand Bucket Company n.d.)

[46] (Matzler, Renzl and Würtele 2006)

I would argue, however, that price confidence can also be defined as to what extent a supplier believes that an offered price is currently favourable.

Price confidence can be low at the lower levels of the pyramid, increasing as we reach the top. It always amazes me how often products and services are undervalued, primarily due to a lack of confidence in pricing.

Stagnant

From experience, our stagnant pricing stemmed from a lack of confidence to increase prices. When we are unsure about the value we deliver, activity within the broader market or concerned about the volume of sales, it can be tempting to leave prices alone rather than risk upsetting something and losing customers. To address stagnant prices, we need to build confidence to have the required conversations with customers or the confidence that we will still be viable even if we lose some customers or if the volume of transactions reduces.

Discounted

Default discounts again stem from a need for more confidence. The salesperson may feel the product is not worth the agreed selling price, and this lack of confidence translates into offering a discount before one has been requested. In my experience, we could be better at judging or understanding how others value our products or services. There may be industry-wide practices that involve discounting, and our lack of confidence in daring to be different can result in us falling into line with our perception of the industry rather than what is suitable for our company. I have seen organizations set up whole processes to manage discounting, creating extra work and complexity to manage a process that might not even be required. Discounts are not just about our confidence in what customers will pay, they are also about internal confidence – can we trust our salespeople to discount appropriately and not leave us with unprofitable transactions? Discounts and confidence, or a lack of it, seem to be inextricably linked.

Competitive

When we benchmark ourselves against the competition on a pricing front, confidence may be either a positive or negative factor. If we believe we have a solid offering to the market, we may take confidence from this and feel more comfortable submitting a bid or providing a quote close to what we believe we are worth. If, on the other hand, we need more confidence in our proposition compared to the market, we may find ourselves overestimating how much value to include to secure the work. When companies are busy and confident about the pipeline, they may decide to price something higher than they usually consider – trying to 'price themselves out' in effect. Sometimes this can backfire and you still win the work, albeit at a higher margin than you would usually achieve. The challenge with competitive pricing is if we do not fully understand what the customer values and are confident in that knowledge, we may be tempted to think that price is the only criterion under consideration.

Dynamic

A dynamic pricing model provides confidence in many areas. The process of establishing the model itself requires an organization to thoroughly understand its economic engine and what drives business. This is frequently a lightbulb moment for organizations, and with it comes newfound confidence that optimizing operations around the economic engine will have a positive impact.

A dynamic pricing model has a built-in decision framework and provides flexibility to sales staff to do what is necessary to secure the business without compromising overall profitability. Rather than needing to sign off every discount, thresholds and rules can trigger a double-checking process, leaving managers confident in providing sales teams with more autonomy.

When there may be doubt about whether or not to offer a discount for a particular transaction, team members can make confident decisions using the model. If they have 'sold' their target of the critical resource that day, week or month, they can confidently offer a price reduction, whereas if they have not, they can equally confidently hold fast with their pricing. Dynamic pricing can be a highly effective confidence boost.

Valued

The beauty of valued pricing is confidence from both sides of the transaction. The customer is happy to pay a premium, as they love the product or service and have confidence in the quality, service and benefit they will derive. There is likely to be little post-purchase dissonance.

On the other hand, the organization is confident its products or services provide value to its customers, understands this value and is therefore satisfied with the prices being charged. These organizations rarely, if ever, discount without purpose. Discounts are part of a strategy to win business or provide opportunities to convert new customers by giving them a 'sample' of the product or service at a lower price.

People

One of the challenges of growing a business is ensuring that the staff you employ are as productive as you used to be when you were delivering the products or services. I know when I used to run a software company, we were less productive once I stopped writing code. There are so many reasons why this might be the case and one of these lies in the engagement of the people in the business.

Gallup has been monitoring employee engagement for over two decades. In its 2024 State of the Global Workplace survey, it found that only 13% of employees are engaged at work in Western Europe.[47] This figure is only 10% in the UK, a 1% drop compared to 2017.

There is a considerable correlation between employee engagement and productivity. The 2017 edition of the same Gallup report shares that engaged workforces are 17% more productive than work groups in the bottom quartile of engagement.[48] It goes on to state:

---

[47] (Gallup 2024)

[48] (Gallup 2017)

> *'... engaged employees produce better business outcomes than do other employees across industry, across company size and nationality and in good times and bad.'*

Running a business with low levels of engagement and productivity is like trying to climb Mount Everest without a team of sherpas.

Jim Collins and his team conducted a long-range study in which they studied the financial performance of Fortune 500 companies over a timespan of at least 25 years. An initial shortlist of 1,435 good companies was eventually reduced to 126. During that period, 11 companies they classified with good performance experienced a transition prior to 1985 and became great; that is, they delivered at least three times the stock market average over a 15-year period. In his book *Good to Great*, Collins shares the things that got them there.[49] One of the most crucial was 'who' is in the business. He talks about 'getting the right people on the bus – and the wrong people off the bus'.

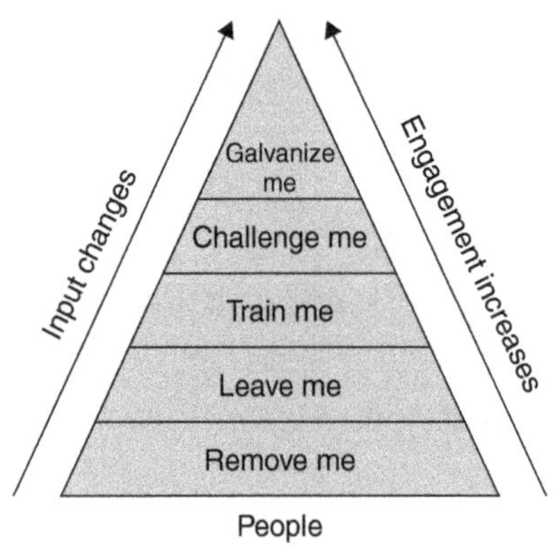

Figure 6 People side of the productivity pyramid

[49] (Collins, *Good to Great* 2001)

Over time, I have observed that people within commercial organizations, and probably most organizations, generally fall into one of five different categories. The categories form a hierarchy, but unlike Maslow's famous hierarchy of needs, where each level is required to move up to the next, I have found that team members generally fit within a given level within a given environment. Put them into a different environment and they might be at a different level. Sometimes they can move levels in the face of extreme pressure.

Level 1: Remove me

At the bottom rung of the ladder is 'remove me'. These are the disengaged team members who are dragging everyone else down. They are often like a cancer within an organization, infecting those around them and wreaking havoc until they are removed.

With a few exceptions, we generally do not act on remove me quickly enough. When I run workshops with CEOs, at least one person in the room admits to having someone on their team whom they would categorize as remove me.

The difficulty leaders often have is that they can feel responsible for this person's poor performance. Perhaps they do not feel they have set the expectations clearly, have not provided sufficient training, or the person has a lot going on in their personal lives, so their poor behaviour is overlooked. If we have condoned or accepted their behaviour for a long time, removing them from the organization can become even more difficult. After all, if we have not told them before, it will be challenging to deliver such bad news suddenly.

Although there are frequent perceptions of HR issues and cost implications of removing people from organizations, the cost of not doing so is rarely compared accurately. Keeping such people on the team extends well beyond the financial. Their mood and demeanour can affect their colleagues. Disengagement is contagious, and it can lower the bar for other members of the team.

Some remove me people are challenging to identify because they can be 'star performers' in their areas of expertise. Perhaps they are a stellar salesperson who consistently meets and surpasses their targets. Yet they leave a trail of destruction for colleagues to fix in their wake, or over-promise to customers and the organization cannot deliver on those promises.

A good question to ask yourself if you are debating whether someone truly is a remove me candidate is whether you would offer them a job if you were hiring now. If the answer is not a resounding yes, you have your answer.

Case study: A remove me saboteur

A medium-sized consultancy client experienced this first hand. Having recently implemented an enterprise-wide combined project accounting and financial accounting system, they recruited a new finance manager. The finance manager struggled to adopt the new system and surely and steadily succeeded in undermining the system's reputation. First, they convinced a new finance director that it was not a good enough financial accounting tool, so they reverted to their previous standalone finance system. This generated a massive amount of work every month to transfer data between the two systems and reconcile the two to ensure the project accounting correlated with the financial accounting. The project accounting system was still used to generate sales invoices, raise purchase orders and process timesheets, expenses and purchase invoices. All this data was then imported into the standalone finance system at each month's end.

Once the finance manager successfully moved the company back into its previous finance system, they started undermining the project accounting tool with the project directors. At each month's end, the project managers were required to estimate the value of the work earned on their projects. The project accounting system provided a facility for them to do this, and then after running a process it calculated the revenue earned in the month. For whatever reason, and I still do not understand to this day, the finance manager convinced everyone that the process did not work correctly and asked them to provide the information in spreadsheets instead. In doing this, they undermined confidence in the new project accounting system, leaving many senior personnel wondering why they had spent so much money on it in the first place.

> The finance manager eventually left the organization. Within two months we restored confidence in the software, retrained all the project managers to use it to calculate their value of work earned, and improved the speed of the month-end reporting as a result. It took far longer, however, to get rid of the two-system status quo that was by this time in place, which drained the productivity of the finance team and led to a need for extra personnel who, once it had been eradicated, were no longer needed.

Level 2: Leave me

'Leave me' team members want to come to work, do what they have always done, the way they have always done it, and go home. They prefer to be left to get on with what they know how to do and are unlikely to want to share details of how they perform their role. Fundamentally, they do not want their world to change. Their resistance to change often comes from a fear of the unknown, although forthcoming retirement or disenfranchised team members can also be a factor.

Leave me is not always a bad thing. Many organizations need people who come to work and get their jobs done, who are predictable and can be relied upon. However, due to the nature of the world in which we live, one that is constantly changing, there comes a time when everyone's role will need to change in some way.

When the organization forces change on a team member who is at heart a leave me, they face a decision. They either adapt with the organization and move up to the next level, train me, or they will ultimately need to move down a level and become a remove me.

Some organizations unwittingly treat many of their staff as if they are leave me team members. Rather than investing in them and providing them with training and development opportunities, they adopt a 'leave alone' attitude. However, leave me works both ways; it can be a challenge for organizations that have leave me employees when what is required are team members who can adapt and change to the environment, and it is also an obligation to keep employees.

A 2019 study from the Sitel group found that 37% of employees would leave their current jobs if they were not offered training to learn new skills.[50] Suppose we consider that the UK Skills Survey of 2022 found that only 60% of employers have funded or arranged training for staff within the past 12 months, and 40% of employers have not.[51] If 37% of the employees in this 40% of companies were to leave their current roles as a result, that is nearly 15% of employees that might be moving jobs due to lack of training.

50 (Schwantes 2019)

51 (Department for Education 2023)

Case study: Leave me until you cannot

I shared a story previously about a finance manager in a medium-sized consultancy. This organization also provides a great example of a leave me team member. This team member had worked for their employer for many years. The company had been acquired by my client, and over time the team members had been required to stop using the current software tools and adopt the new company-wide project accounting system. This individual found learning the new system incredibly difficult. Thankfully, a phased introduction meant they only needed to know some parts of the software tool initially. Over time, however, more and more functions were required, and when they were finally required to complete their monthly reports within the new tool, it all became too much, and very soon afterwards this individual chose to retire.

In some situations, intrinsically leave me team members suddenly become train me. One of these situations is when an organization faces a crisis. Under these circumstances, previously change-averse team members can suddenly become galvanized to respond to the sense of urgency. This can help them move outside of their comfort zone.

We saw many examples of this during the Covid pandemic. I have lost count of the number of clients who have shared examples with me. Working practices they had been trying to change for years were suddenly changed overnight and accepted by everyone. An NHS trust had been wanting to implement a seven-day-a-week shift pattern for its occupational therapy team and had not felt able to do so. During the Covid pandemic, however, they were required to move from a five-day-a-week pattern to a seven-day-a-week pattern almost overnight, and it was accepted without challenge.

In other examples, companies that have had to make redundancies have found the team members left behind who might previously have been described as leave me have stepped up and asked how they can do more to save the company.

In Kotter's change model, he espouses creating a sense of urgency to encourage the adoption of change. He is perhaps most famous for the highly readable book, *Our Iceberg is Melting.*[52] However, in *Leading Change* he talks in more detail about the role of urgency within his eight-step process for change:

> *'A higher rate of urgency does not imply ever-present panic, anxiety or fear. It means a state in which complacency is virtually absent.'*[53]

It is dangerous for organizations when they have leave me leaders. These leaders filter communications and ideas; anything new and threatening may not be shared. These leaders block engagement, effectively creating a barrier between their team members and the rest of the organization.

---

[52] (Kotter and Rathgeber, *Our Iceberg is Melting: Changing and Succeeding Under Any Conditions* 2006)

[53] (J. P. Kotter 2012)

Engagement strategies that try to work through these leaders will ultimately fail, and instead, rather like when a tree falls across a road, routes around them will need to be found for new ideas to be successfully implemented.

Level 3: Train me

Our 'train me' team members are the fuel in our organizations. If you want your car to keep running, you need to invest in fuel; if you want your organization to keep running and evolving, you must invest in training your team. Train me team members want to learn new things and keep developing. Counterintuitively, however, these team members do not always ask for training. However, if you treat a train me team member like a leave me team member, you can expect they will eventually find employment elsewhere. It is a bit like a cactus – you can neglect it for a long time and, ultimately, if you do not water it, it will die, whereas if you provide it with occasional water, it flourishes. While some will be very up-front, many will quietly carry on with their roles, almost like you would expect a leave me person to behave. Inside, however, they secretly yearn for development opportunities.

The correlation between those employees who learn on the job and those who love their jobs is well documented.[54] Once you identify these team members and invest in training and development opportunities for them, you will earn their loyalty, and they will carry your organization through the required evolution and development into the future.

[54] (Murphy 2018)

Occasionally I come across leaders who are concerned that investing in their people might be counterproductive in that they will take the development and then leave for new pastures. Whenever I come across this perspective, I am reminded of a well-known Peter Baeklund joke:

> *CFO asks CEO: 'What happens if we invest in developing our people and then they leave us?'*
>
> *CEO: 'What happens if we don't, and they stay?'*

If the cost of training is considerable, there are always ways to ensure that companies enjoy the benefit of the training through training agreements, which ensure employees do not terminate their contract for a period of time. If they do, they refund the cost of the training. I believe we need to look at creating working environments that our teams want to be part of, and invest in their future rather than worrying that our hard-earned money will be lost if people leave.

Case study: Excel train me

During one client engagement, I provided interim finance manager services for a multidisciplinary consultancy that ran multiple software tools across its organization. The finance team had the unenviable job of reconciling numbers across various tools at each month's end. I had been struggling somewhat to engage the finance team members, despite it being year-end, with a range of challenging obstacles in front of us. I found myself working long hours while the rest of the team left promptly at 5:30. One day I spotted two members of the team reconciling two spreadsheets of information together. It was such an inefficient use of time that I was compelled to intervene. I showed them how to compare two lists in Excel using the VLOOKUP() function to find missing entries and verify that values across the two sheets were the same.

Doing this saved two people hours of work; instead, one person could achieve the same result in minutes. It was also the turning point in our relationship. From then on, both team members started asking me if I could suggest a faster way to complete mundane tasks.

Level 4: Challenge me

Now and again, we find someone in our organization that runs at a faster rate. Not only do they complete work quickly, they come back and ask, 'What next?' These team members can sometimes push leaders to their limits, keeping them on their toes. In some situations, leaders can run out of tasks to keep their 'challenge me' team members engaged.

These team members are often the source of new ideas, keen to press ahead and implement them, often without having considered all the consequences. Challenge me team members love coming up with new ideas and improving how things work.

Leaders who are not themselves challenge me types can find themselves being pushed outside their comfort zones or needing more time to correctly evaluate the tsunami of ideas being generated. Managing a challenge me person is a bit like guiding your luggage trolley down a ramp at the airport and having to pull it back to prevent it from running away ahead of you and banging into the people in front.

Challenge me team members tend to be rare. Deployed effectively, they can drive progress in your organization, and one thing you can be sure of is that if they are not challenged, they will almost certainly leave for somewhere they will be challenged.

I was fortunate to attend a conference a few years ago at which Jim Collins was the speaker. He shared a story about one of his famous messages: 'putting the right people on the bus'. I forget the organization; however, it was a rapidly growing international company, and he had the opportunity to speak to the CEO. The CEO explained that his people strategy was essentially to find the best people, or in Jim's language 'the right people for the bus', and then work out what jobs to give them. This is, of course, almost the reverse of what most organizations do. Instead, we work out what roles we need to fill and then find people to fill them.

Case study: Challenge me or lose me

I have personal experience of being a challenge me team member. My first post-graduation job was in a PR agency. As someone who has always wanted to learn and constantly looks at how things work to improve them, I became frustrated with the slow pace of change. I was eager to progress and create an impact, and wanted more autonomy. When I had my appraisal, I was given all kinds of reassuring feedback that my aspirations matched my manager's. However, when it came to it, I still felt micro-managed and needed to constantly check first to make decisions. One day, I realized that despite all the promises, it would take a long time for my manager to relinquish control, so I found myself looking for a new challenge elsewhere.

Level 5: Galvanize me

Galvanize is a process of covering a metal, such as iron or steel, with a protective zinc coating by dipping it into molten zinc, or by electrodeposition. It creates a metal that is more resilient and protected against rust. To galvanize someone means to cause them to take action.

Organizations create 'galvanize me' team members when they create environments where team members are emotionally connected to the organization. This could be the result of an alignment between an individual's internal values and beliefs and those of the organization, or due to the level of psychological safety and appreciation individual team members experience.[55] When these conditions exist, team members may make it to the top of the pyramid.

The number of team members who are galvanize me is even smaller than those who are challenge me. They are the people in your team who, if you were to cut them through the middle, would have the company name written through their centre, like a stick of rock. These team members uphold the company's values, come what may, and can experience despair if those around them do not. They can feel lonely and like they are the only ones who care.

Galvanize me can be a temporary place; over time, if insufficient others join them, or the organization fails to provide them with the right support, they can give up.

These team members can be found at every level of the organization. They are not only found in the boardroom; identifying them can be valuable. They might be the people collecting the trolleys in the supermarket car park, the receptionist or the warehouse manager. These team members understand what the organization is about and will do everything they can to protect it and its future while solving customer issues creatively. Astute organizations ensure their galvanize me team members are deployed strategically, with opportunities to apply their skills, experience and passion for the organization effectively.

Hopefully, we will all encounter a galvanize me team member sometime in our lives. If we have not found one in our organization, we may have enjoyed interacting with one in another context.

---

[55] (Edmondson 2018)

Case study: Mum's birthday

There is a 2018 Cadbury's advert, 'Mum's Birthday', recently revived, that illustrates this beautifully. A young girl is collected from school late, by her apparently harried mother. On the way home, as they pass the newsagent's shop, Mum receives a phone call. While she is answering the call the daughter enters the shop and asks to buy a bar of chocolate: 'It's for my mum.' The shopkeeper sees the mother outside talking on the phone and pulls out a bar of Cadbury's Dairy Milk. The girl opens her purse and proceeds to lay out a plastic coin and two buttons on the counter. This is where the shopkeeper shows he is a galvanize me. Rather than explaining that he needs real money, he indicates that it is not enough, and she proceeds to hand over a plastic medal, a ring and, rather reluctantly, a small toy horse. He nods and hands over the chocolate bar, and then, as she is about to go, he prompts her to take her change, the small toy horse. As she leaves, she says it is for her mum's birthday.

In this example, the galvanize me team member appears to be the shop owner. It is therefore easy for him to make that split-second decision to act in the way he does. It is when an organization has succeeded in creating a larger network of galvanize me team members who all know they are empowered to make such decisions that the organization can really start to fly.

Julian Richer, chair of Richer Sounds, writes in his book, *The Richer Way*:

> *'... the most important and most neglected people in any business are the employees. And the most important – and most neglected – of these are the ones who actually deal with the customer.*
>
> *I've found that if a business has problems with customer service, it comes back to how that company treats its staff. The product is irrelevant: the key to success is always how you treat people so that they are motivated and productive and, in turn, treat your customers well.'*[56]

Managing different people

In his highly acclaimed book, *How to Win Friends and Influence People*, first published in 1936, Dale Carnegie writes:

> *'Personally I am very fond of strawberries and cream, but I have found that for some strange reason, fish prefer worms. So when I went fishing, I didn't think about what I wanted. I thought about what they wanted. I didn't bait the hook with strawberries and cream. Rather, I dangled a worm or grasshopper in front of the fish and said: "Wouldn't you like to have that?"'*[57]

---

[56] (Richer 2001)

[57] (Carnegie 2018). Case Study Courtesy of Bob Gorton of 'Hard Had Business Advice.'

This point beautifully illustrates a concept: what motivates me does not necessarily motivate you. Each level on the people side of the pyramid is essentially a different form of motivation. Leaders and managers are recommended to consider in which of these levels their team members reside at any point in time.

Understanding this is fundamental to understanding the levels of engagement and the different management styles that various team members might need. We must remember that team members will move from level to level over time, depending on various factors, some of which may be within the organization's control, and others will be external and potentially outside of their control.

Case study: Nora Sands from leave me to galvanize me

In 2004 and 2005, the celebrity chef Jamie Oliver launched a campaign to revolutionize school dinners. He was galvanized to take action against the declining standards of school dinners within British schools. He recorded a four-part documentary in which he taught cooks at Kidbrooke School in the Royal Borough of Greenwich how to prepare nutritious, low-cost food rather than simply heating chicken nuggets and chips.

The formidable head dinner lady at Kidbrooke School, Nora Sands, could initially be described as leave me as she and Jamie clashed frequently. Nora appeared to initially resist Jamie's attempts to deliver a more healthy menu. She has since divulged that her resistance was due to her own lack of confidence; she was being asked to order ingredients that she could not pronounce, let alone spell.[58]

However, Nora eventually became one of Jamie's most ardent supporters through the campaign, travelling with him further afield as he set up pilot schemes in Lincolnshire and Dorset, connecting local schools with pubs, hotels, restaurants and local farmers.[59]

Jamie's passion galvanized Nora to pick up the mantle, with the series leading to a national campaign, Feed Me Better, to improve school dinners across Britain. In March 2005 the Government announced a commitment to invest an extra £280 million in school dinners over three years.[60] Sadly, however, in 2007 Nora resigned her role, citing frustration that none of the extra money or training for staff promised by the Government had materialized.[61]

Let's look at the differences involved with managing team members at different levels of the pyramid.

---

58 (Middleton 2006)

59 (Wikipedia – Jamie's School Dinners 2012)

60 (Matthews 2005)

61 (Manson 2007)

Remove me

At the lowest level of the pyramid, the remove me team member will likely require significant amounts of management time. These team members will ideally be under some form of performance management. Consequently, they may experience low levels of autonomy, with regular communication likely to comprise conversations seeking to understand issues, addressing concerns and reviewing performance. It is expected that traditional reward systems have not worked or will not work, and therefore consequences may be more appropriate than rewards. There may be a desire to invest in training in the form of soft skills, although this is unlikely to be successful.

Leave me

At leave me, management may feel like there is little input required. There are likely to be relatively high levels of autonomy as team members know what to do. However, if the organization is undertaking any change programme, levels of autonomy are probably lower, and micromanagement may be involved. Within the status quo, communication may take the form of routine and scheduled meetings or reviews; otherwise, communication may be required when dealing with exceptions rather than the norm. This can be a dangerous place to be, as these team members may feel neglected somewhat if everything is going as expected and fires need to be put out elsewhere. Using reward systems to motivate these team members to be more productive may be challenging, as their motivation lies in the status quo. It is unlikely there will be requests for training, or training may be offered and not taken up.

Train me

By the time we reach train me, the level of autonomy may drop as team members learn new skills and push into new areas. There will likely be more management or peer input required. In addition to any regular scheduled meetings or reviews, there is often more ad hoc communication initiated by the team members as they may need clarification on unfamiliar decisions or actions. Where train me people are being developed, this is often a sufficient reward in itself; however, if their desire to develop has yet to be recognized, extrinsic rewards will likely become more critical to prevent disengagement. Training is, of course, a key feature at this level. It can be essential to ensure that training is relevant and appropriate, not training for training's sake.

Challenge me

The challenge me team member is characterized by high levels of autonomy and a desire for independence if it does not already exist. These team members will want to make their own decisions. As such, decision frameworks are a helpful management tool for these team members, providing as much autonomy as possible and ensuring consultation where exceptions occur. If there is insufficient autonomy, challenge me team members may grow frustrated. It may feel like a constant flow of communication from these team members asking what else they can do or whether they can get on with their next great idea.

Managers who prefer a structured communication cadence may need to increase the frequency and identify ways to deal with email overload. Left too long without input, challenge me team members may become challenging as they may be prone to go it alone and get on with whatever they feel is important. These team members gain much of their reward from recognition or the intrinsic reward from the challenges. They will be keen to take advantage of opportunities to develop their knowledge or skills and will likely be judicious in their choice of training opportunities.

Galvanize me

Our galvanize me team members can be some of the easiest to work with, needing some of the lowest input levels. Typically, these team members experience high levels of autonomy as they intrinsically know what to do in many situations, using the organization's core values as their North Star. Communication with colleagues and managers is likely open and transparent, with high trust levels. These team members will value recognition, although that may come in different flavours; some may enjoy peer recognition, others public recognition, and others private recognition. Recognition can be particularly important if they are not in senior management positions.

Galvanize me team members often enjoy the intrinsic reward of executing their roles and living the organization's values. Any extrinsic rewards provided on top of this will likely have an exceptionally positive impact. Such rewards will be most effective when they are tailored to the individual. Corporate reward schemes that treat all team members the same are unlikely to be valued; as Marcus Buckingham and Curt Coffman outline in their book, *First Break All the Rules*, fairness does not equal sameness.[62]

A significant danger for leaders is that these team members still need some input and can often be overlooked. Managers often spend the most time with their least productive team members, supporting them, while their colleagues who can already do the job are neglected. Buckingham and Coffman also make the case that managers should, conversely, spend the most time with their most productive team members.

62 (Buckingham and Coffman 1999)

Process

Getting the process right is how organizations can reduce the number of people required to service customers or service more customers with the same number of people (i.e. without increasing overheads). And yet, all too often, the process is one of the last things organizations invest time in.

The challenge with process is that unless it is documented in some way, whether through written instructions, a storyboard, a video or a flow diagram, there is no process. Yes, there are agreed ways of doing things; however, as soon as you have more than one person completing a task, if there is no documentation, you have two different approaches to achieving the end result. Typically, you end up with as many different ways of doing things as there are people who carry out the task. Some of those people will have found shortcuts, workarounds or improvements; others will not have done so. Each person will have learned the job from someone different, so everyone gets trained slightly differently.

To improve a process, you need to know what is happening. Once it is documented, it is easier to see the issues, and multiple people can be involved in making improvements.

If the process is clearly documented, and everyone is doing the same thing, there are considerable benefits to an organization. New ideas or improvements can be shared, and the benefits can be seen not only by one person but also by all those who carry out the same tasks. An excellent way to increase productivity is to find the best way of doing things and then repeat, repeat, repeat.

There is an evolution in the development of a process, as seen in the five levels of the process hierarchy in Figure 7 below. Understanding where you are on the hierarchy is helpful as it helps inform what steps are required to get to the next level.

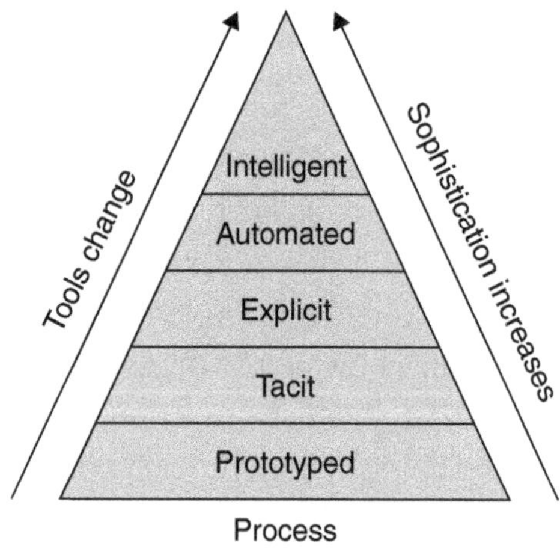

Figure 7 Process side of the productivity pyramid

Level 1: Prototyped

The starting point for all processes is prototyping. During prototyping we are doing things, checking the outcome, refining it and then redoing it. Many product-based organizations understand the concept of prototyping, as most of the products they sell have been through a prototyping process. However, for some reason, they do not always think about prototyping all the processes that surround their products.

The feedback loop during prototyping is fast. Try something once, evaluate the outcome and then refine it immediately. Prototyping works best when one or possibly two people are involved in a process – the instant feedback leads to improvements.

Organizations go through prototyping at various times. When the organization is established, everyone is learning how to do everything for the first time. When an organization launches a new product or service or enters a new market, there will likely be time spent prototyping new products, services and processes to bring these to the marketplace. Not many organizations routinely review their processes and re-prototype improvements before rolling them out across the business. Generally, this kind of prototyping is triggered by a significant event, such as an acquisition, a merger or a new software system. This is a missed opportunity, as processes are like shrubs. While they need trimming annually, the gardener cuts a third of the dead wood out every three years to make room for new growth while maintaining the overall shape. If we think about our core business processes like this, we would embrace prototyping more routinely.

Clues that you are prototyping:

- The process changes with every run.
- One or two people are operating the process.
- The feedback loop is short.

- There is almost no documentation on how the process is completed, as it is held within someone's head.

Case study: Hockey club

A hockey club decided to automate its volunteer onboarding process. The existing process involved the club administrator creating an entry in the DBS (Disclosure and Barring Service) system and then sending an email to the volunteers asking them to complete it. This email included all the steps they would need to go through. This included completing the online application and clicking on a link to book a time to meet with the welfare officer to verify their ID. The calendar booking link also asked them to send electronic copies before the verification meeting. The same email contained information on how to complete the safeguarding training, how to reclaim the cost of this training and what to do with the certificate.

The compliance was poor. Too much information in the email resulted in the process taking weeks and the administrator having to follow up and chase people, which took several hours a month.

The new process involved creating a customer relationship management (CRM) system and automating much of the process. The new process sent only as much information as was necessary for each step, and once that step was complete it sent another email with further instructions.

The safeguarding training and the DBS checks were separated into different communications. A weekly reminder was automatically sent, tailored to whichever step of the process the volunteer had reached. For the first few weeks every email that was sent was reviewed to check that the rules that had triggered it were correct. When the volunteer did not respond as expected or raised a question, the wording of the email was adjusted to remove any ambiguity and to address the question raised within the text for all future volunteers. Within two months the level of compliance had increased from around 60% to over 80%.

This is an excellent example of how prototyping can take place. Almost every time the process ran, the outcome was checked, verified and, if necessary, improved.

Prototyping is a helpful step to include when thinking about automating any process. By starting with a low-tech prototype, many assumptions can be verified at low cost and refined before they are automated.

Level 2: Tacit

Many organizations are rife with 'tacit' processes. These are processes that exist in people's heads. The typical evolution of a tacit process starts when a team member joins an organization. They are trained to do their job and operate the relevant processes. Sometimes they write notes on how to do it while learning. Those notes eventually become redundant; they know how to do it without checking. This is when the process has become tacit.

If this team member is subsequently asked to train another team member, they will typically replicate the process they went through. This method can be inefficient. As the process resides in their head, things can be missed during the transfer of information. When the new team member discovers missing information, they must refer back to their trainer. Alternatively, mistakes are made, they are spotted and the missing information is transferred.

A tacit process is almost like having no process. It is contained in the heads of individual team members, and each team member will frequently have a different view of how the process is carried out.

Tacit processes make increasing productivity difficult. If you cannot see a process, it becomes challenging to discuss it, understand the parts that could be made more productive and ultimately improve it.

Many organizations have pockets of tacit processes within their operations. Frequently they have documented key business processes that are directly concerned with their product or service delivery, making them explicit. If we take the case of an organization that makes clothing, for example, there will be a pattern for each garment, a cutting list that shows all the pieces of cloth to cut, and the zips, buttons, threads and labels to be included. They will have worked out how much fabric is required, how long it will take and the best way to assemble the garment. All this will be explicitly documented because they need to make lots of copies of the garment, and they need to be of consistent quality.

Compare that, for example, with the process of dealing with a customer complaint for one of the garments. This is less likely to have been described with such rigour and is therefore held as tacit knowledge. It is usually left to a relatively senior member of the team, one who knows what to do and for whom the process is stored in their head.

Organizations with too many tacit processes can struggle with productivity if other factors, such as high staff turnover or large teams, are also present. Where there are high levels of staff turnover, corporate knowledge can often be lost along the way, as people leave the organization, and the handover is not long enough to securely transfer all the tacit knowledge. Over time the reasons why things are done (or not done) a particular way are lost, and the organization has to relearn through making mistakes.

Where there are large teams, such as large customer services teams, large sales teams or large teams of consultants, the tacit process means that the quality of service is likely to be hit and miss. Suppose there is no consistently documented way of delivering a product or service. In that case, the sheer fact that many people are involved in the chain means significant variations in the level of services provided will exist. This can harm an organization's reputation.

The case for consistency is clear; a 2014 study by McKinsey of 27,000 American consumers found that effective customer experience journeys are more important than exceptional ad hoc interactions.

'...measuring satisfaction on customer journeys is 30 percent more predictive of overall customer satisfaction than measuring happiness for each individual interaction. In addition, maximizing satisfaction with customer journeys has the potential not only to increase customer satisfaction by 20 percent but also to lift revenue by up to 15 percent while lowering the cost of serving customers by as much as 20 percent.'[63]

Case study: Blind manufacturer

During an Unblock Audit™ for a large blind manufacturer I spoke with several people who were involved in processing orders from customers. The company operated its own bespoke software, which had evolved over many years. As I completed the discovery conversations, it became clear that there were several different approaches being used for what was essentially the same task. Consequently, there was significant variation in the quality and output of the different individuals. Upon further investigation I learned that a different person had trained each team member, and there was no formal documentation on how to use the company's software system. It highlighted the challenges organizations face when a process is held as tacit knowledge.

---

63 (McKinsey & Co 2014)

Level 3: Explicit

Contrary to tacit, 'explicit' processes are documented. They are usually the result of a significant investment in time to understand how things need to happen and the documenting of this. Documentation may take many forms, of which flow diagrams are a common type. Written instructions or procedures are often placed in lever arch files, put on shelves and then rarely read. Other organizations use video tutorials, storyboards or visual prompts to help document their processes and procedures.

Product-based companies already do this well for their products. As I have already mentioned, if a clothing company wants to be successful, it will create a production pack that outlines precisely how to consistently make a size 10 version of a particular garment. A food production company will have a recipe for making its signature sauce. Everything will be documented: the quantity of each raw ingredient, how they need to be prepared, the order to mix the ingredients, the temperature and the length of cooking time. Rarely, however, do they pay this much attention to the processes surrounding their products. These processes include taking orders, shipping, sending invoices, receiving payment, placing purchase orders, receiving goods, etc. These processes are just as important in their impact on overall productivity and need the same treatment.

When we conduct our Unblock Audit™, we map out a high-level process map for one of the critical business processes. In many cases this will be the first time this process has been made explicit, and the number of variations that team members have will become clear as the discovery conversations progress. In one case, a team member who had worked for the organization for over seven years commented that he had never seen the whole process mapped out like that and had no idea of all the steps that had to happen before and after the part in which he was involved.

An explicit process helps everyone understand the objective or end result. It is a visual representation of current practices, whether good or less than ideal. It is the basis for improvement and can be used to brainstorm, discuss and challenge existing working methods.

Case study: Accountancy firm

An accountancy firm I know invested heavily in documenting all of its processes. When new staff members joined the team, they were asked to spend their first three months learning how things worked and to make recommendations about improving the processes. A recruit noticed that files saved to a client folder were named haphazardly and suggested they could be stored in the format yyyy-mm-dd-NameOfFile, which would help to find things because they could quickly be sorted by the date of creation, even if they were subsequently amended. This idea was well received; consequently, the procedure notes were updated, so everyone started to operate the new way of working.

Any organization wishing to make more of its processes explicit must invest some time discussing how things are done and finding ways to document this. Once confirmed, it can be shared with a broader audience, and the conversations required to improve them can begin.

When conducting an Unblock Audit™, I usually work one-on-one with team members to gather the level of detail required to unearth many opportunities to unlock productivity. However, it can be helpful to give feedback on the overall process to a cross-functional team and talk through the opportunities for improvement. Almost always there will be dissent in the room, where someone in the team will dispute the viewpoint of another department. The facilitator's role in this is to let the conversations take place, give both departments the space to share their own experiences, and ask questions to help them reach common ground. If the facilitator can generate ideas to overcome any identified challenges, then so much the better.

Case study: Audiovisual company

An audiovisual company struggling to make money seized the opportunity to document its processes. Most of its work was project-based, with sales transactions involving conducting a survey, designing an audiovisual solution, procuring the equipment and installing and testing it.

> The company reviewed several recent projects and pulled together a standard checklist of tasks that needed to be completed for each project and the questions that needed answering to identify which optional tasks had to be completed. It then went on to document instructions describing each step's procedures. As it grew and took on new staff members, it could scale with relative ease and increased its productivity by 150% over three years by following this strategy.

There are many schools of thought that constraining people by being too prescriptive with process documentation can create automatons, curb creativity and cause jobs to be less meaningful. My perspective on this is different. When provided with the right level of process documentation, many questions that would otherwise clutter up our team members' time and attention are answered, so they have more energy to devote to delivering products and services brilliantly. For example, suppose I do not have to go to someone and ask how to deal with a particular customer complaint, and I can see that the value of the compensation is within my authority limit. In that case, I am free to delight the customer and provide an excellent customer experience the first time they contact me. If this is not the case, I can get caught up playing piggy in the middle between the customer and someone more senior, and my role becomes meaningless and frustrating.

The trick with process documentation is to pitch it at the right level for the people in your organization to provide sufficient structure and guidelines without hampering creativity and the opportunity to deliver exceptional customer service.

Level 4: Automated

Once we have made processes explicit, the next level of productivity is to automate our processes. When we can automate, we can achieve much higher levels of productivity. Automation takes many forms. On the factory floor, automation might be a CNC (computer numerical control) machine or a robot on a production line. In the back office it might be electronic processes that take repetitive manual processes and codify them so they can be executed with minimal human intervention. This might be a macro that formats an extract into a usable spreadsheet, replacing many keystrokes with a single click to save time on a daily task, or an event-driven workflow that understands when the next stage has been reached and automatically sends out relevant communication.

Marketing automation is an excellent example of an 'automated' process. Many companies are investing in marketing automation systems that respond to events as potential customers engage with marketing activity. For example, when someone leaves their details on a website, they receive an automatic email with information relevant to their enquiry. Or if a customer puts something in their shopping basket and does not check out, the system sends them a reminder email to prompt them to complete the transaction.

While marketing has embraced automation, there are many areas of organizations where automated processes still need to be explored.

Case study: Clothing manufacturer

Many years ago a clothing client embraced automation and, by doing so, cut their lead times by over five weeks. Each season (autumn/winter or spring/summer), the buyers would arrive to view the new collection and send a bulk order for their many stores. These spreadsheet-based orders were then keyed into their homegrown order processing system. Once the orders were on the system, they could calculate how much fabric needed to be purchased to satisfy them. Purchase orders were then raised on the fabric manufacturers, some of whom had lead times of many weeks. The clothing company's challenge was that keying in the buyers' orders took six weeks. This added six weeks to their lead times, and if they were unable to manufacture and ship the whole order before the end of the season, they were left with garments the buyer would no longer accept, so lost money.

This was a process ripe for automation, and we worked with them to 'read' the spreadsheets into their database automatically, allowing a process that took six weeks to complete within three days.

Consequently, the fabric purchase orders could be placed over five weeks earlier than had previously been achieved.

One of the temptations I often see is organizations that rush to automate before they have completed the previous levels. Automating during prototyping can be costly unless the person prototyping can also create the automation. This is rarely the case, as large ERP (enterprise resource planning) systems usually require technical expertise to implement business requirements.

Automating before making a process explicit is also fraught with problems. The challenge here is that if we share a process verbally and expect someone else to automate it, things will be lost in translation. Unless the same person with the implicit knowledge of the process is also responsible for automating it, it is foolish and potentially expensive in terms of both time and money to try to automate it. At the very least, there needs to be an adequately documented specification of what needs to be automated, having considered all possible permutations and combinations.

During software implementations, we often see 'customizations' requested to automate processes within the software. These are usually poorly done for two reasons. The first is that they are often automated before the software is implemented and in use, which means that often things are automated that never need to be automated, or the automation is based on an ill-informed understanding of how the software will operate once it has gone live. The other reason is an inadequate understanding of the business process before trying to automate. This often happens when the process has not been thoroughly explored and documented before the programming required to automate commences. It is typical to discover that several scenarios are missed, so the automation works for some scenarios and not others.

To avoid this, when documenting the process before automation, a varied sample of transactions should be 'walked' through the established process to ensure that all possible scenarios are covered. This step is rarely completed due to a perception that the time involved is not justified. However, when it is missed, the consequence can be that, during testing, new test data identifies different scenarios that were not previously considered, so the development needs rework, which is costly and can cause project deadlines to be missed.

Case study: Manufacturer

During the implementation of a new ERP system, a client's bespoke sales process required heavily customized software. The lack of robust process documentation during the requirements gathering resulted in many new scenarios coming to light during user testing. This resulted in the change requests going backwards and forwards between the testers, the consultants and the developers over many weeks, contributing to a delay in the project going live and significant additional costs for the organization, both in consultancy fees and the cost of their team members in having to redo the testing repeatedly.

When a process is automated without first making it explicit, an organization's other challenge is that it will create technical debt over time. There will be no documentation describing how the automation works, and future changes or amendments, often involving new team members, will need to work out how something works first to change or improve on it. Technical debt is not a metaphor; it costs real money. New developments take longer and have more problems, and any bugs or troubleshooting takes longer than it should.

Case study: Building materials

A client with a legacy software system that was heavily customized experienced a problem with the sales prices within the system. It operated in a fiercely competitive market where all its customers had their own project-specific prices. The issue with the pricing module resulted in their confidential customer-specific prices becoming common knowledge within the marketplace, seriously affecting their brand reputation and jeopardizing business. However, the problem was complex to track down, and nobody in the organization knew how the pricing module worked, so resolving it took a long time (weeks), and all the while the organization's reputation was being undermined.

Level 5: Intelligent

'Intelligent' process can cover two different scenarios. At its simplest, intelligent process is where there is a process for improving processes. With this step, all the hard work involved in making processes explicit or automating them can be retained over time. This is because, despite documenting the process, it is natural that new ideas, new staff and new technology will cause the process to be amended or need to be amended over time. Without a process for formalizing these changes, the process will revert to being prototyped and then tacit, and the productivity gains will once more be undermined.

A process for improving the process can be created in several ways. The starting point is to create a culture where improvements and suggestions are actively encouraged. For example, this could be via a suggestion box, a regular forum or a suggestion email address.

Each process needs to have an owner, the person responsible for 'looking after' the process and any changes that might be required. This team member would then periodically review the process to see how it might be improved. A suggestion might trigger this or it might be a periodic review. The process owner must determine how frequently such a review might be required. For some processes, annual, bi-annual, or three-yearly reviews might be sufficient; however, more frequent reviews might be appropriate in a rapidly changing organization or market.

RACI (responsible, accountable, consulted, informed)

Documenting a RACI for each process helps us understand the team members involved in any review. RACI is an acronym that describes different team members' roles within a specific context.

Responsible: Who is responsible for this process? – this is the team member who does the work to ensure that any changes to the process are incorporated and shared. There may be more than one team member responsible.

Accountable: The person ultimately responsible for the process – the process owner. This team member is the ultimate approving authority and arbiter in case of any disagreements. This should be one team member.

Consulted: These people need to be consulted about any changes. They will have a vested interest in the process because changes may affect their areas of expertise. These team members are subject matter experts. When putting together a cross-functional team to review a process, all those invited would be within the 'consulted' category.

Informed: These people are kept up to date on a one-way basis. In the context of a process, this will typically involve all those involved in executing the process or who receive the output that have not already been consulted. There may be many team members that need to be informed.

When reviewing the process, the best option is to involve a representative of all those currently operating the process, aiming for a cross-functional team to ensure all perspectives are represented. These team members should be listed under 'C' in the RACI matrix for the process.

If responding to a suggestion, it might be that only the suggestion needs to be discussed; for a periodic review, it would be more usual to review the whole process. During these reviews, some helpful questions can prompt the conversation:

- Is this step still required?
- Does it still make sense for this role to complete this process step?
- Is there anything here we can automate?
- Would moving this step earlier or later in the process improve anything else?
- What might be the benefits of this suggestion?
- What might be the unintended consequences of this suggestion?

It is, of course, essential that any changes to the process following the review are agreed upon, and they are implemented and communicated to all those who need to know. The documentation for the process should be updated to reflect the changes.

The updating process is an overhead within any organization, yet it is crucial to maintain any productivity improvements that have been delivered and maintain a healthy growth in productivity over time. Getting this global process right can turbocharge an organization to continually improve its productivity.

Artificial intelligence (AI)

The other intelligent process is where AI is employed to improve the outcome of processes over time. For the vast majority of businesses I have come across, this is a relatively high aspiration, and automating critical business processes is a higher priority than looking at AI. For those ready to investigate and leverage AI, it is worth understanding more about this topic.

AI is an umbrella term for computer software that mimics human thinking to perform complex tasks and learn from them. Until 30 November 2022, and the launch of ChatGPT, which heralded the start of the AI revolution, for most businesses what was most valuable was machine learning (ML), a subfield of AI in which algorithms trained on data sets are used to produce adaptable models to complete various complex tasks. ML queries large datasets to find patterns that can be interpreted. ML does not learn from its mistakes – it requires humans to change how it solves problems.

It is worth remembering that the basic assumption when using ML is that what has worked in the past will work in the future. So, for example, if you have ten years of sales data and want to use it as the basis of a ML model that could help you predict where to target your sales and marketing resources, this data is only helpful if you expect future customers to behave in the same way as previous ones. In a rapidly changing landscape, historical data sets become less valuable. This challenge has faced economists since the financial crisis of 2008; none of their models works any longer, so the decades of data they have previously used to predict what will happen in the future are now redundant.

We are now entering a new world of AI. ChatGPT represents a step-change in its capabilities. It heralded a new breed of generative AI; that is, AI models that are able to use the vast data sets upon which they have been trained to create content in response to questions or 'prompts' from humans.

One of the challenges with applying AI or ML within organizational processes is a need for more knowledge about what can be done and how to do it. While this technology is now starting to become mainstream, it is not new, and a 2019 article in *Forbes* magazine provided some examples that are still relevant today:[64]

Automate routine tasks: ML can become an additional IT team member, monitoring security, performing audits, checking the status of scheduled jobs and generating reports. These tasks can consume hours that could be used on more strategic activities.

Gauging risk more effectively: Managing risk is complex, and few organizations do it well, and those that do rely on managers to make decisions based on limited data. ML can help provide a more complete understanding of a business's risk profile, particularly in relation to fraud, errors and loss prevention.

[64] (Expert Panel, Forbes Technology Council 2019)

Improving personalization: AI and ML are helping advertisers learn where to target their advertising spend and remove much of the guesswork involved, allowing marketers to get to know their target audience more thoroughly. Historically, ML was targeted at many IT-related applications; these days, all aspects of a business can leverage ML. A recent article in business.com shares several areas where ML is helping increase productivity.[65]

Leaner manufacturing: ML apps can spot potential breakdowns before they happen, thanks to sensors on production lines. This can help improve planned maintenance, reducing the downtime of production lines and thereby increasing capacity overall.

More efficient logistics: Sophisticated global positioning system fleet tracking systems can now maximize vehicle capacity, saving money on fuel, which has reduced the cost of each delivery.

More effective decision-making: ML apps linked to CRM systems can help customer services agents and sales reps prioritize deals using tools that qualify leads, predict the deal size and even the time to close.

ML is a specialist area, and there are different routes to adopting it within a business. One is to engage a data scientist to look at your data and work with you to leverage it and use it for ML. The other way is to look for ML apps that integrate or work with your existing technology and use these to get started. If you are replacing software tools, it is worth looking at what AI/ML functions the new software options provide.

---

65 (Fairlie 2023)

With the advent of generative AI, a wide range of tools have become accessible to anyone on the internet, and you no longer need to be a data scientist to take advantage of them. With a modest amount of training, anyone can draft compelling marketing copy, analyse and summarize documents or write minutes of meetings almost immediately. Within the space of a year, early AI models that created images from text have developed from producing somewhat quirky images, to photo quality images that are difficult to discern from the real thing.

The role of tools

Something we often do not consider is that frequently tools are agnostic of process. An excellent example of this is the task of knitting a cardigan. The process is to knit two fronts, a back and two sleeves, and then to stitch them together. However, the tools that are used can vary. We can use knitting needles, a manual knitting machine or a fully electronic, automated machine. The process does not change; the tools change.

Sometimes the procedures within the process change when the tools change; that is, the step-by-step instructions might change depending on the tool in use. When we look to change the tools, particularly with automation, it can be helpful to review the process to see whether it makes sense within the context of the new tool.

This is particularly common when implementing an ERP system. Business processes that have historically been largely manual are often highly customized and bespoke. When the tools available are inherently flexible, we can find ourselves creating processes that a less flexible set of tools might have prevented. Not all processes we design are necessarily the best process we could adopt. Therefore, it makes sense to stop and think when changing the tools. Does the process also need to change?

I often see cases where adopting a new tool creates an opportunity to review processes, and this does not happen. The result is often an overly complex set of customizations to make the new tool work with the old process when, in fact, the original process might have been adjusted to fit the standard process offered by the new tool.

Prototyped

Our tools here are often simple. It may be a pencil and paper or a spreadsheet. We are working out how the process needs to operate at this stage. We create documents to capture information; we draw our ideas out on paper, log information in a spreadsheet and establish whether our thoughts will work in practice. When prototyping, the simpler the tools, the better. We need flexible tools so those prototyping the process can adjust and amend the process without any specific technical knowledge. The danger here is that prototyping tools often become the tools for running the process over the long term, which is not always the right approach.

Tacit

There may be a variety of tools at tacit level. In the early days of a process, the tools are likely to be similar to those involved in prototyping. Spreadsheets and their modern equivalents are common tools for capturing progress through a process. We might see paper documents shared across departments. As we have discussed previously, the variable process at tacit means that the tools in use will likely allow on-the-fly adjustments to documents, which must be edited before they are sent.

In more established organizations where there may be a central system, it is also possible to have tacit processes around the primary tool. This may occur when the tool has existed for many years and nobody now knows what sits behind some of the rules and logic. Knowledge of the system is no longer documented. It is transferred verbally from team member to team member, often leading to errors or missed opportunities about how a tool can be used most effectively.

Explicit

The act of making a process explicit can help us to see quickly which tools are in use. While documenting tacit processes is unlikely to require a change in the tools, it can allow us to use the tools we have more effectively. The process of making it explicit brings to our conscious mind the reality of what is taking place.

Such an exercise can highlight the many spreadsheets lurking undetected within our processes. Spreadsheets, which are not subject to the same rigorous development testing of systems developed in other programming languages, are often rife with errors. A 1987 study by Brown and Gould of the IBM Thomas J Watson Research Centre, asked nine experienced spreadsheet users to create three spreadsheets each.[66] Despite being particularly confident that their spreadsheets were error-free, in reality 44% contained errors. In fact, spreadsheet accuracy theory tells us that the likelihood of there being an error in our spreadsheets is anywhere between 7% and 81%, with the number increasing with more complex spreadsheets and the fewer the people who have reviewed them.[67] If nothing else, a by-product of making processes explicit can be facilitating a conversation about whether a different tool might be more appropriate.

When using flow diagrams, different shapes or colours can be used to visually differentiate which tools are used for the various steps in a process. It can be tricky to use colours alone, as when team members are colour-blind this hides a layer of information from them.

I have also seen situations where making a process explicit has highlighted that different team members are using inconsistent tools to complete the same step in a process. While one person might make a phone call, another might check a website to obtain similar information. When documenting the tools in use, we can identify current best practices and help all team members use the same tools.

Automated

The tools we use to automate processes vary widely. It might be a CNC machine, a factory floor robot or a workflow engine in an ERP system. These days, no matter the level of sophistication of your chosen tool, there is almost always a

---

66 (Brown and Gould 1987)

67 (Sheetz and Kruck 2001)

way to cut out some of the need for human intervention to automate parts of a process.

Within spreadsheets we can create macros to execute a series of keystrokes at the press of a button, which work far more quickly than any team member could possibly achieve.

Online tracking systems (e.g. Smartsheet, monday.com, Airtable, Asana) often include the ability to create notifications or execute steps when an event occurs. For example, when a follow-up date arrives, sending a notification to someone to check on the status, or changing the status based on other information that is added to the row.

CRM systems can be used to automate the sending of bulk messages to customers or suppliers. Rather than sending individual personalized (or impersonal) emails, they can be added to a CRM, and then personalized emails can be sent en masse to a broad audience.

Data transfers between systems that involve running a report, exporting the data and then importing it into another one can nearly always be automated these days, either via one of the many tools available on the internet that allow different applications to speak with each other, or by setting up scheduled jobs that run periodically to perform the task. As far back as 1999, I wrote a piece of software that allowed a bill of lading to be produced on an office printer or emailed to a customer from a transaction created initially on an AS/400 mainframe computer.[68] Rather than waiting for the half-hourly batch job to print the bill of lading, the

---

[68] Bill of Lading: a legal document issued by a carrier to a shipper that details the type, quantity, and destination of the goods being carried.

document was available within a minute or so, saving time and, in the case of a container ship, significant expense if the document was preventing the vessel from leaving the port.

Intelligent

When we think about AI in the context of intelligence, the level of sophistication increases yet again. Here we are concerned with vast data sets and ML engines that can take the rules we have provided and perform actions far more quickly and potentially with greater accuracy than any team member.

These engines are now widely available for different applications and often can integrate with your existing technology. Some examples include:

- Fathom: a plug-in for Zoom that transcribes meetings and provides a concise summary of the discussion and outcomes without the need for a team member to take minutes.
- Next-generation AI tools can help generate stories, articles, emails, tweets and other written artefacts such as ChatGPT, Second Brain AI, Tome and Jasper AI.
- In the data analytics space, the ability to streamline and automate reporting on large data sets is supported by tools with varying levels of AI-powered analysis, including Plus AI, Polymer, MonkeyLearn and Power BI.
- In the marketing space, we find tools that help streamline the competitor and customer monitoring process. Brandwatch Consumer Intelligence enables you to understand your customers better and see where your brand fits into the market, while Brand24

monitors your and your competitors' brand across the web and analyses conversations in real time, providing opportunities for companies to manage their reputation more effectively.

Part 3

Finding Untapped Productivity

Conducting an Unblock Audit™

It is one thing knowing that we could improve our productivity; it is quite another knowing how to go about it. It is a challenge that often prolongs inertia. The approach I share has worked reliably in every organization in which I have consulted. It does not matter what kind of company it is. They could be selling widgets, providing consultancy in education, providing PR services or financial services; this approach has always resulted in a significant list of areas to tackle.

We need to conduct an Unblock Audit™ to uncover the opportunities for greater productivity. To be successful, it is essential to structure this audit properly and to observe some basic rules. One of the main concepts to embrace is that this is the start of a journey of discovery. If we had the answers, this audit would not be required, and our productivity would be exceptional.

Picking the right person

It is essential the right person or people conduct the audit. If you use multiple people, then two is a good number, and they should both participate in all aspects of the audit.

Refrain from being tempted to divide and conquer to get there faster. The best people to conduct the audit are those who can speak with people at any level of the organization. They need to talk to those at the top and those on the shop floor (metaphorically speaking, if there is not a physical shop floor). Individuals who can think quickly and flexibly are an advantage; the critical requirement is deep curiosity. They will need to ask many questions and be interested in the answers. If they are generally creative, that is a bonus, as there will be lots of opportunities to solve problems during the audit if they are.

Using someone outside the organization is, without question, the best option because they can come in and ask all the dumb questions without fear of embarrassment or becoming embroiled in any politics. However, not every organization has the luxury of being able to do this, so the next best option is to use people who are sufficiently senior to have a good understanding of the 'big picture' without being too senior that everyone is scared to say anything. There is a distinct advantage to being from 'outside' of the company or department, hence an effective strategy is to find two people from different parts of the organization who can work together to ensure that somebody 'fresh' is always involved wherever they are deployed.

From here on in, I will refer to the person or people conducting the audit as 'the facilitator'.

Discovery requires naivety

The most successful style for the facilitator to adopt is to be naive. If you engage an external facilitator, they are generally naive simply because they do not know your company. When you use internal people, they can struggle to be naive, so they must almost 'pretend' they do not know anything about what happens, to avoid making assumptions.

Facilitators need to bring a questioning and curious mind to each discovery session. Any existing knowledge must be put in a jar, left on a shelf and only used to seek clarity. It can be easy for an in-house facilitator to skip steps or questions because they think they know the answer. This is to be avoided, and an in-house facilitator may need to explain that although they might know the answer to some of the questions they will ask, they would like them answered as if they do not know the answer. Even when you know something about the topic, you must pretend you do not. Be like a child who is seeing everything for the first time.

Having a structured conversation

The biggest fear I encounter when conducting an Unblock Audit™ or mentoring others to do them is the fear that we will not be able to do it properly or that our team will not correctly express the problems. The solution to this is making every discovery conversation a structured conversation. To achieve this we need a framework within which to operate.

It can quickly lose its way if we try to hold a discovery conversation without a framework. Inexperienced facilitators will struggle to keep the conversation on track, and before we know it we will have gone down multiple rabbit holes and time will have passed, and we will not have captured what we need to know. Using a framework speeds up the discovery process, which, after all, is what we want to achieve.

A framework is even more critical when working with team members who do not realize what they know and struggle to explain things. It can help them understand the context of what they are sharing and see how it fits into the whole.

It is essential to be flexible when using a framework. While its job is to focus the conversation, it is by its very nature narrow, and there will be lots of good stuff sitting on the fringes or slightly outside the framework. We need to capture all that good stuff as well, so the trick is to allow the framework to scaffold the conversation, to enable the conversation to move outside the framework when required and then to use the framework to refocus everyone again when that is the right thing to do.

Thankfully, there is one framework that applies to every business I have ever encountered.

The order to cash (O2C) process exists in every profit-making and most not-for-profit organizations. Some educational institutions do not have a straightforward O2C process, so they may require something different. For example, a state primary or secondary school might struggle to outline an O2C process.

Working on the basis that if you are reading this you are running or responsible for a significant part of a commercial organization or something very similar, there will be an O2C process. And that is where the journey starts.

The O2C process

This is the core process in most organizations. It is the process that generates cash flow and, therefore, is one of the most essential processes. It starts when a customer places an order and ends when the cash has been collected. It also includes all the steps involved in delivering the goods or service to the customer. In many cases, these happen before the customer pays; however, cash collection may occur before the delivery if your organization does not operate credit terms.

A simple O2C process might include the following steps:

- Customer order received.
- Order processed on an internal system.
- Deposit payment (or full payment) may be taken.
- Order fulfilled – in a stock-based business, this may involve picking it from the warehouse, ordering it from your supplier or making it to order. For a services-based business, it may be scheduling the work and ultimately completing the service.
- Order delivered – either physically or electronically.
- Invoice raised.
- Cash collected.

Mapping the O2C process

The first task of our Unblock Audit™ is to map a high-level O2C process for the organization. The facilitator needs to work with a senior leadership team member, if not the CEO or managing director, to draw a picture of the process. This does not need to be a polished affair; in fact, I often grab a piece of A3 paper on my first day in a project, go through the process and then use that same piece of paper throughout. So do not overthink this step. While important, it should take less than an hour to complete, and the result will be rough and ready.

Using the basic outline described above, the facilitator needs to draw a box for each process step. If the process is as simple as the one in my example, there will be seven rectangles in the map, with arrows connecting them. However, processes are rarely as simple as this, and almost every company I have ever worked with has been at great pains to tell me how their organization is unique.

There are often decisions to be made during the process. For example, is the product the customer has ordered in stock? If yes, pick and ship; if not, raise a purchase order to get some in. These scenarios need to be reflected in the process map.

If the facilitator is not experienced in process mapping, there are a few fundamental rules to note:

- Process maps show at a high level the steps involved in a process.
- They describe the flow of a transaction through the organization to completion.
- There will be sub-processes involved that are not part of this map (e.g. procure to pay (P2P)); do not be tempted to include those, or it will all become too complicated.
- High-level process maps must avoid getting into the level of detail reserved for procedures.
- If there are many different product or service offerings, it may be necessary to map multiple O2C processes.
- Out of preference, start with the process that generates the most significant proportion of revenue.

Who to speak with?

Once you have a process map, working out who you need to speak with is the next step. For each box on the process map, you need to identify who is involved in that step. Write their name next to the box. In some cases you will have multiple names. For example, you may have numerous salespeople or multiple customer service executives. It is rarely necessary to speak to each of them. You can often talk with just one. There is, however, sometimes a benefit in speaking to two people who do the same role. This could be somebody really good at what they do and somebody less effective. Or you could select somebody relatively new to the role and someone who has done it for a long time. Managers should guide the facilitator as to who can best explain the procedures in place behind each box on the process map.

There are a few traps essential to avoid:

- Ensure you speak to those performing the role rather than their managers. While the managers can make a valuable contribution, speaking with those who carry out the day-to-day operations is crucial.
- Identify a broad range of people to involve. If too few people are involved, and they need to cover a wide range of responsibilities, the conversations will extend over a longer time, and fewer perspectives will be considered.
- It is important to include senior leaders. Their contribution will be more strategic and outcome-focused rather than operational, and it is crucial to understand this to make sense of the detail that will be collected.

- Where possible, hold one-on-one conversations before you undertake any one-on-many conversations. Facilitating a discovery conversation with many people is more complex and always more successful if you have gone through the details in a one-on-one conversation first.

Scheduling time

So, we have our process map, and we now have a list of the people with whom we need to speak to understand more about what goes on in the organization. We now need to book time in their diaries. Each discovery conversation will likely take between one and a half and two hours, so allow sufficient time. If you book two hours and only take an hour or 90 minutes, you will be 'gifting' time into the team's day.

Conversations with finance team members can often take longer than two hours. This will depend upon the structure of the finance team; however, here you may end up talking with the same person about multiple topics, so schedule these as separate meetings to give both of you time to recharge and reflect.

When I consult with an organization, I complete all the conversations within a couple of weeks. If the period extends beyond this, it can be harder to hold all the information gleaned in your head.

It is tempting to schedule a single meeting with both people who have been identified to talk about a particular step in the process. Start with one-to-one conversations before conducting any one-to-many conversations. It takes an experienced facilitator to manage the dynamic when two other people are involved in the conversation. It is easier to encourage a single person to elaborate freely. When two people are involved, many complex relationships can interfere with the conversation. Fear of saying the wrong thing, stating an opinion, and not knowing enough. When you are working one-to-one and you are clearly 'naive', many of these fears disappear.

There is one situation where it makes sense to conduct one-to-many discovery sessions. In a company with multiple similar and different divisions, there will be a lot of repetition across divisions. It can, therefore, be helpful to engage with a group of identical role holders across multiple divisions to identify what they do that is the same and what differences exist. However, before attempting this, you must have gone through the same one-to-one conversations with everyone involved in the process within one division. Then you can go into a one-to-many discussion from a position of knowledge rather than naivety, and explain what you have learned and ask for similarities and differences.

Case study: Multi-discipline consultancy

A multi-discipline consultancy operating in the built environment asked me to help them with an Unblock Audit™. They were sure each division would have different ways of working. There were ten divisions:

> cost management, project management, architecture, civil engineering, etc. To be most time-efficient and effective, I suggested we conduct the initial audit with structural engineering team members. Once we had completed all the team members involved, we conducted discovery conversations for the remaining nine divisions simultaneously. We did this by function, so we spoke with all the business unit directors on one call, a project manager from each division on another call, the project assistants on another, and so on.
>
> In this way we could quickly identify what was the same and different for each division without holding nine times as many conversations.

If in doubt, the recommendation is always to work one-on-one. And never conduct a discovery session with someone whose manager is also present.

Knowing what to expect

Many team members when told they are going to be asked all about what they do will start to feel some anxiety. We want everyone to feel relaxed and speak freely during our discovery conversations; after all, they may have some great ideas to increase productivity and are waiting to be asked!

To help this, I usually ask the director who has commissioned the audit to email all who are due to participate. I provide them with an introductory message from me, which outlines what to expect and aims to put them at ease. A copy of the template can be found here in the resources available for this book 👆 https://resources.amandasokell.com

This message contains the following information:

- Why – the purpose of our conversation, why we are meeting, and who has asked the facilitator to conduct this audit.
- When – the period during which the conversations will take place and how long they are likely to take.
- Where – if you are doing this face to face, explain that you will come and sit by their desk. If this will be virtual, ask them to join you from their normal workplace.
- What – I usually give them some idea of what they might like to think about before we speak. There are some suggestions in the template; for example, lists of reports they use, spreadsheets they use and things they find frustrating. I always add that, if life is too busy, they do not need to worry as the time we spend together will be sufficient to capture everything I need.
- How – I explain that I will bring a high-level overview of the business process and ask them to talk me through their role and show me what they do. It would be great if they have particular examples they can hold back to go through with me.

I also mention that I might spot something that would help them do their job faster or more efficiently and that I hope the time spent will be beneficial to both of us.

And then... I also explain how I will use the information they share and what it will be used for. I explain that anything they share will be in confidence and anonymous, and they will be credited with the ideas if they have any great ideas.

Quantify the opportunity

It is all well and good learning about how things work in the organization; however, when we later start to analyse what we have learned and think about where we might find productivity gains, we need help in prioritizing the ideas. During each discovery conversation, the facilitator will likely uncover many existing challenges in how team members work.

Case study: PR company

During an Unblock Audit™ with a PR company, the sales director mentioned that her account managers were spending vast parts of their day chasing the delivery teams for updates on their client projects. This was a big challenge for her because the result meant the team was not talking to clients and selling new business. Nevertheless, when she mentioned it, she did not elaborate, and it seemed a somewhat 'vague' sense that this was a problem that needed further exploration. I asked her how much of the account managers' time was spent chasing. Initially, she responded that she did not know, and together we eventually established that it was three to four hours a day. Five days a week. For 20 account managers. It was an incredible revelation that each of the 20 account managers lost 50% of their working week chasing other teams for updates.

As we can see from the above example, this almost 'throw-away' comment resulted in a realization by the sales director that she was losing the equivalent of ten FTE members of staff on unproductive inter-departmental communication.

It is, therefore, important that the facilitator makes sure they quantify all the challenges that are shared during a discovery conversation. It is rare to come across something this significant; however, it never ceases to amaze me how much waste lurks in every organization, only for it to come to light when we go through these structured conversations.

Quantifying the opportunity can also be helped with some key non-numeric questions. One that I always use is 'tell me in three words what [company name] does'.[69] This question helps when evaluating the understanding of 'promise' in the organization. Occasionally team members struggle to answer this question, so I try to keep it as open as possible rather than directing them how to interpret it.

69 Hat tip to Chris Hughes for this great question.

Case study: Metal recycling

During an Unblock Audit™ for a metal recycling company, I spoke with a team member who attended a remote site where the metal was processed for onward transport. It transpired that this process was highly profitable and could only be conducted when the team member was on site to operate the machinery. However, due to the limitations of the software system they were using, he needed to come back to the office at the end of each day to process transactions on the system. During the audit we identified that this was costing the company thousands each week, as his day was being cut short by 90 minutes, five days a week. The solution was relatively inexpensive. It involved providing the operator with a laptop and a mobile internet connection so the transaction could be processed at the remote site rather than requiring a journey back to the office.

Great questions to ask to help quantify the challenge include:

- How often does it happen?
- How long does it take?
- What is the cost or impact?
- How many people does it affect?
- What could you be doing if you were not doing this?
- What is the cost of the waste when things go wrong?

We are seeking to capture time that could be saved, waste that could be reduced, missed opportunities, the cost of mistakes, the cost of compliance and the risks associated with not doing things that should be completed.

Overcoming uncertainty

When we ask team members to put numbers on something, frequently they tell us they do not know or cannot say. There is something about making a general statement; however, when asked to be precise we suddenly start to second guess ourselves and consider the problem is not quite as big or as bad as we might have made out.

So, how can we overcome this uncertainty?

By providing boundaries, we can help identify more accurate estimates. When you hear someone say, 'I don't know,' give them an answer. This might sound a little strange; however, although we might not know the correct number, we almost always know the wrong one. So, try saying, 'Does this happen every day?' Or, 'Does it take an hour?' When faced with an incorrect number, team members will often use that to work out an accurate number. They will know that it is more or less than the number you have suggested, and hey presto, before you know it, they have come up with a reasonably accurate estimate – they know more than they believe.

I think the feeling is a bit like reading an overwhelming menu – there is so much choice you cannot choose anything. If you restrict the options, suddenly it is much easier to find something you would like to eat.

Facilitators must ensure that they gather data in every discovery conversation to back up the commentary.

Spreadsheets are your friends

It is a rare discovery conversation when a spreadsheet does not come to light. When I say spreadsheet, we are not restricted to simple sheets these days. Some organizations use sophisticated online platforms that are essentially glorified spreadsheets and have built-in workflows, automation, etc. They might be insulted if you refer to them as spreadsheets. However, no matter what the software is called, if it looks like a spreadsheet, treat it as a spreadsheet.

There is a wealth of information lurking in spreadsheets across most organizations. Even where there is an enterprise-wide software tool (such as an ERP), there will also be spreadsheets. This is particularly true in an organization that is growing quickly, as the ERP rarely keeps up with all the new products and services, so spreadsheets grow up in the cracks to store all the information that will not go in the ERP. It is one reason I call them Polyfilla® systems.

Towards the end of our discovery conversation, I usually ask each team member to show me all the spreadsheets they use. I ask which ones they use the most frequently and ask them to send me copies of them all. It is a bit like having an amnesty – at our local hockey club, we have a ball amnesty every summer, inviting members to return the many missing hockey balls that have been 'lost' during the season.

Putting together an inventory of all the hidden spreadsheets usually identifies at least one document that proves to be mission-critical and that, to all intents and purposes, is largely invisible.

Make a note of the columns of information being collated, and in particular look for duplicates of the same information being maintained by multiple people in multiple sheets.

If team members cannot think of their most commonly used spreadsheets, you can also ask them to go to their recent files list, as this will show the documents they have opened most recently. Sometimes this quickly jogs their memory.

Historical data

Another critical part of the discovery process is to gather historical data. This can help understand how an organization could be more productive. Historical data can paint a picture that shows how life changed when certain decisions were made. If you think back to the Covid pandemic, we saw the impact of lockdowns on the number of cases. If you go back now and look at the historical data, you can see the point at which decisions were made and the impact of these, albeit with a slight delay.

Historical data that may be helpful include financial information, turnover, cost of sales, net profit, debtor days, creditor days and other key financial metrics. Also beneficial are records of customer complaints, returns, refunds, proposals submitted, sales conversion information and so on. Gather any of this information that you can obtain for use later.

Possibility

Discovery conversations are about more than just the facilitator learning about an organization and gathering data. They are also a huge opportunity to explore new possibilities within a forward-thinking discussion. When I have conducted a few discovery conversations, I often start to generate ideas that might improve processes. Rather than waiting until I have completed my audit, analysed the results and reported back to the leadership team to share new ideas, I broach them with the team member in the moment. I usually phrase these ideas, 'I wonder if…' and wait for their thoughts. Sometimes they help me understand why my suggestion would not be practical. Other times they are cautious and need to think about it, and now and then I see a spark of excitement in an eye, and I know that the seed has been sown and they will be looking at what they can do to make that possibility a reality.

Most team members are constrained within their world of 'what is' and are not encouraged or inclined to stop and question their current way of working and to consider alternatives. However, when asked directly how they could improve things, they often have ideas they have never shared with others.

Understanding that we are embarking on the first stage of a change project, we need to use every opportunity to start opening our minds to new ways of working, so beginning in these very early conversations makes sense.

Now and again I encounter a team member who needs help to think about how they would improve things. This is why I give every team member I speak with three wishes. I explain that I have a magic wand and they have three wishes, and they can wish for anything they want within the framework of the project. That is, I cannot help them win the lottery! There is something about stepping into a magical world where anything is possible that allows even the most reluctant participant to come up with at least one idea of something they want to change. In the few cases where they do not use all three wishes, I explain that they can come back to me in the coming week if they think of something they would like to add to their wishes. Using this question right at the end of a discovery conversation is essential, almost as a 'final question'. Doing this can help you understand which of the many topics of conversation you have covered are the top three priorities for this team member.

Helpful questions for exploring possibilities include:

- I wonder if it would work?
- How would you ideally like it to work?
- If we could get it to do… would that be an improvement?
- If anything was possible, what would you like to see happen?
- I have seen it done this way elsewhere. Do you think that would work for you?

Sowing the seeds

During any change programme, some team members will embrace the change, some will get there eventually and others will actively resist the change. Sometimes team members need time to get used to a new idea. Discovery conversations are, therefore, a fantastic opportunity to sow the seeds of new ideas or changes that are coming. In the same way that seeds do not germinate overnight, some will germinate quickly when given water (e.g. cress in some tissue paper), while others need to be kept in just the right conditions and can take many weeks or even months to sprout. Some seeds need a 'shock' to the system, such as being put in a refrigerator to germinate.

Entrenched ways of working can take time to change, commonly when team members have worked for an organization or in a role for many years.

Sometimes the facilitator will quickly identify new ways of working or be informed about planned company changes. Sharing these during discovery conversations can be an excellent way to help the most change-averse team members start to think about what those changes might be and how they would apply to them. It is generally accepted that when team members are involved in coming up with ideas, they are more likely to embrace change. Therefore, discussing ideas or changes in this way can help team members feel involved in shaping the ideas and will assist when it comes to implementing these ideas further down the line.

This works when the discovery conversation is open, and there is psychological safety. When the facilitator creates a space where the team member feels able to share anything, the good and the bad, they are also most receptive to new suggestions, provided they are framed correctly. Sticking to the theme of curiosity and naivety, the facilitator will likely receive the best results by asking questions rather than making statements.

- 'I wonder if we could try…'
- 'I wonder if doing… might help?'

'What if' questions are also helpful.

- What if we did not do that?
- What if we did this first?
- What if someone else was doing this piece?

These are all good examples of questions that sow the seed of possible future changes.

Become a collector

As facilitators, we must collect ideas to share in new contexts or with new people. There are very few new ideas. Most so-called inventions are, in fact, taking an existing idea and applying it to an alternative situation or application. This is a vital role of the facilitator. Facilitators will come across ideas within an organization that could be used elsewhere. If they are curious about the world, they will also come across ideas from outside the organization that could be applied within.

Testing new ideas

When testing new ideas with team members, it is generally better to start by sharing them with one person at a time and establishing that the concept is well received before sharing them with a larger group. This can be particularly helpful if the facilitator is from outside the organization. It is better to 'fail' quietly with an idea in a one-to-one conversation than in front of a big group. It is also an excellent way to sense which team members are most open to new ideas and which might require more support to adopt new ways of thinking and working. Testing the same concept with multiple people in a one-to-one conversation can be helpful.

Jim Collins expresses a similar idea in his book *Great by Choice*.[70] He uses the concept of firing bullets before cannonballs. He writes that successful companies test new ideas on a small scale before spending lots of time and energy implementing them.

The phenomenon of group think often threatens idea acceptance. Group think can shut down a new idea before it starts to take hold. It only takes one vocal or opinionated person to declare it will not work, and if that person has sufficient standing in the organization the rest of the team will agree. It is a courageous team member who speaks out in favour of an idea that a colleague has already shot down.

When the facilitator has tested an idea a few times, sharing in a group can be done successfully as it comes with existing support. The ideal scenario is to frame the idea in such a way as to indicate that several team members have already given their support to it. Alternatively, the facilitator may have had support from existing team members to gather data or evidence to support the new proposal.

It is never too early or too late

While the ideal time to sow seeds of new ideas and test new ideas is during a discovery conversation, there is always time to do so. A facilitator who goes back to a team member following their discovery conversation, perhaps due to a future discussion, will help that team member feel valued and involved. We all appreciate when others take an interest in what we are doing, so when somebody comes back to us, the following day or even a week later, with a suggestion or

---

70 (Collins and Hansen 2011)

idea that has occurred to them since our conversation, we will likely give them our attention.

Recording the discovery

When I facilitate discovery conversations, I record them. Before the Covid pandemic, this involved me recording a voice message. At the time I used a Livescribe pen, which recorded the audio while I took notes. It is a nifty device that, when you touch the notes page, the audio automatically plays what was being said at the time. During the Covid pandemic I recorded Teams or Zoom calls when everything went online. These days there is a wealth of plugins; for example, Fathom for Zoom, which will transcribe your call for you, and is invaluable for a facilitator.

In addition to recording, I always take notes. As a student I learned to touch type, and it has been an invaluable tool. Even if you cannot type, capturing screenshots or screen clips and adding some notes to remind you will save you time trawling through a lengthy real-time recording.

It is vital to 'flag' the data you collect within your notes for speedy retrieval. I tend to use OneNote for my note-taking, which provides various ways of tagging information. I can search the notes later for a specific tag and gather all the relevant information in a single view.

Updating the map

As you speak with people and participate in discovery conversations, you will discover that your process map is not entirely accurate. When steps are missing, the facilitator needs to annotate the map so the new information is included for the following conversation. Without doing this, you will spend valuable time in several discovery conversations rehashing what is wrong with the map, despite already being aware.

During their various conversations, the facilitator will uncover other processes, for example, the P2P process, which includes the steps involved in placing an order for goods or services from a supplier through to paying that supplier. Record to report includes the steps involved in generating financial and management reports within an organization, and these steps are often additional procedures on top of general day-to-day business activities.

It is helpful for the facilitator to sketch these processes roughly for their personal use as they uncover the steps. Despite the conversations being focused on O2C, these other related processes will inevitably be discussed and should be addressed.

Case study: Global pharmaceutical

I was engaged to conduct an Unblock Audit™ for a global pharmaceutical company that wanted to better understand the processes involved in its clinical research functions. The company had been on the acquisition trail, and it therefore had several offices on both sides of the Atlantic that were fundamentally doing the same thing, albeit in different therapeutic areas.

I started in the UK and spent a few weeks working around the clinical research organization to understand the various business processes. Once I had this information, I took a whistle-stop tour of three other sites in North America. I was only able to do three sites in a week because I had a good map of what happened in the UK. Rather than seeking to understand from scratch, I was able to have conversations about what happened in the UK and asked team members to indicate what was the same and what differed. This was helpful on two counts. First, it significantly condensed the process. Rather than spending several weeks in North America, I gathered the required information in a week. The second benefit was that the North American team members learned from me what their UK counterparts were doing. In some cases this included sharing new ideas and best practices, which they then adopted. By the time I arrived at the third and final US office, I could share what three other offices were doing, so any exceptions to that needed more justification.

Part 4

Solutions

Which Lever to Pull?

Pulling the productivity levers

We now understand what productivity is and what levers we can pull to increase productivity, and we have conducted an audit of our operations to identify the areas where we have the most significant opportunities to adjust what we are doing to increase our productivity.

However, if the audit is anything like the ones I have conducted, there may be a long list, perhaps several pages long, of possible places to start, and selecting the best starting point is essential.

Pulling the right lever first

I have seen examples where lots of time and effort has been put into fixing issues, say within the process side of an organization, in an attempt to increase productivity. All of this with the best intentions; however, had the organization looked at price first, more than half of the steps in the process might not have been required at all. It is crucial, therefore, to understand which levers provide the most extensive improvements or can act as the most significant catalysts to overall productivity growth.

A good starting point is to categorize all the ideas that have been generated, all the magic wand wishes and ideas that came out of the discovery sessions and tag them as either price, people, process or promise. It can be helpful at this stage to look at the overview and note which lists are the longest, as this can provide insight into particular levers that might be higher priorities.

The following recommendations apply to any organization identifying its productivity culture as problematic or systematic. If your culture is traumatic, the right lever is the one that fixes the trauma first. Because trauma often results in a loss of cash or people, any opportunities you have identified that will help increase cash or reduce the departure of people are the ones to focus on first.

Promise

If we think back to the productivity model, the three levers of price, process and people can be presented as circles in a Venn diagram, situated within an overall circle called promise. It stands to reason, therefore, that fixing the promise is the first and most important lever. When I run workshops for CEOs, one of the exercises I ask them to complete is to draw out the process of making a cup of tea. It is a relatively simple process that most people recognize, and yet, due to many personal preferences, it can result in some highly distinct results. Only once they have completed the task do I share the missing link and let them know the purpose of the cup of tea. Once they know for whom they are making the tea and the context, many of their process maps are suddenly not as relevant.

So, aligning all your team members on the promise and ensuring it is the right one is a good starting point. When you review the answers to the question 'tell me in three words what this company does', you see an eclectic mix of responses with no overall picture; it is a good indication that the promise is poorly understood within the organization. At the very least, your organization would want to be at the we know level on the price side of the pyramid. If this is not the case, this is probably the first place to start.

This is not a marketing book; it is a book about productivity, so I do not propose at this stage to go into detail on how you can clarify your promise, other than to say that done well it can be one of the most significant investments you make in your organization. A well-articulated promise can become the 'hook' upon which many other things are hung.

Case study: Blue Rocket accounting

Blue Rocket is a firm of accountants in Kent. Some years ago it invested in an exercise to understand its promise and eventually came up with a way of delivering its accountancy services, which lent itself to the space theme. As a result, it went on to name its teams after planets, its receptionist became CapCom, and many of its services were themed around space. Clients receive Magic Stars and a Milky Way bar upon their company's birthday anniversary. Everyone in the organization understands the promise, and it all fits together as a cohesive whole.

Price

Price can be another helpful lever to pull early in your strategy to improve productivity. This is particularly true if your pricing is currently at stagnant, discounted or competitive. Moving an organization away from these pricing strategies (if appropriate), aligning behind a pricing strategy based on the organization's critical resource limitation, and using dynamic pricing can stimulate a significant improvement in productivity and profitability.

If you are an organization that includes any element of overhead absorption or the labour of staff members in your cost base, my strong recommendation is to re-evaluate the cost of your products and services after removing this. One reason for suggesting this is that there is usually a lot of effort and sometimes time-consuming process involved in calculating the required information to add this into the cost model. By taking it out, much of the overhead process can be removed.

Take, for example, a kitchen manufacturer. Each unit has a bill of materials and a certain amount of machine and labour time to assemble. Rather than working out the time to build the unit, and hence the cost of the labour, it would be more helpful to know the cost of the bill of materials. This will provide the value added for the unit (sales price less cost of materials). The only other information required is the number of units of the CRL that the unit consumes during the sales transaction. This might be its volume in the delivery truck, the number of hours on a particular machine, or the hours of labour if this is the CRL (and here is a hint: in a business that makes products it is rarely the labour). Simplifying the costing model in this way can reduce several time-consuming business processes, and sometimes these processes get in the way of quoting customers, as they add significant delay to the process.

Once the costing exercise has been completed, the result is an understanding that the product will generate £x of value added and use y units of the CRL. An organization needs to know no more than this to accurately price its products and services and sell them for the highest value added possible.

Case study: Housing association

A housing association had been making losses for 18 consecutive months before being introduced to the concept of CRL and dynamic pricing. A 90-day programme involved the leadership team identifying the CRL, communicating this across the organization and re-evaluating its pricing. At the end of the 90 days, the company delivered a small profit for the first time in 18 months.[71]

---

[71] Case study courtesy of Bob Gorton of Hard Had Business Advice

Process

The third most effective lever to pull is the process lever. One of the objectives of pulling the process lever is eradicating unnecessary processes and process steps and optimizing what is left.

One concept that needs to be addressed when looking at the process is to focus on the whole system; that is, the process, rather than looking within a department or steps in isolation. For example, if something takes three hours to complete, one hour with person A, one hour with person B and one hour with person C, and we want to bring that down to two and a half hours, it does not always mean that everyone will spend less time on the process. For example, it might be that the way to achieve it is for person A to spend 1.25 hours, person B to spend one hour, and person C to spend 0.25 hours. A proposal such as this can be thrown out before being properly discussed, based simply on the premise that person A has no spare capacity, or the department in which person A works has no extra capacity. We need to focus on the whole system and see how we can redeploy people to ensure that the overall process is optimized, without allowing office politics or personal fiefdoms to get in the way.

It can be tempting to think purchasing or replacing an ERP system will fix all your process woes. However, this is unlikely to be the case. An ERP will instead exaggerate the issues, allowing them to happen faster and with more significant impact than any manually operated processes.

Case study: Kitchen manufacturer

During the Covid lockdown of 2020, a client discovered that nearly £800,000 of revenue was tied up within its ERP system because a system administrator put on furlough was no longer 'easing' transactions through the system. It turned out there were several business rules frequently broken by orders going through the system. These were not documented and were, therefore, invisible to the business. The system administrator had been fixing the data and ensuring that they progressed, and thus, in their effort to 'help', they had in fact been silently contributing to a time bomb. When they were not there to fix the data, the transactions got stuck, never quite making it through the system to be invoiced and the cash collected, even though customers had received their orders and they had been installed.

To prevent a recurrence of this, the client wanted to have all steps and business rules documented so they were clear, and then put in place quality checks at each stage to ensure that all transactions had correct data to start with, thus negating the need for anyone to 'fix' the data retrospectively. This relatively straightforward step improved productivity instantly.

Process automation is an opportunity for many organizations and can generate significant productivity growth. Even small automations can make a huge difference quickly.

With today's technical landscape, even those who do not consider themselves technical have been able to use automation to improve their productivity. While I am not advocating unstructured automation, it is interesting to see how companies are carving out productivity gains in discrete parts of the organization.

Case study: Workerbee recruitment

Inspired by a workshop on the opportunities for using AI such as ChatGPT within the business, one of Workerbee's co-founders decided to automate how new temporary staff were onboarded. The existing process was highly manual. Inquiries from new workers were added as a new row to a tracking spreadsheet. The operator would then send them application forms and aptitude tests to complete and documents to sign, ask them to provide proof of right to work, and update various columns on the spreadsheet to indicate when these were complete. When inquiries arrived overnight or at the weekend, the applicant experienced a delay until the office reopened the following working day. In a competitive market, candidates often apply for multiple jobs at the same time, and Workerbee would lose out on the best candidates where there was a delay in progressing an application; this often meant working long into the evenings and over the weekends to ensure that candidates were constantly engaged.

To resolve this, the co-founder asked ChatGPT to write the required Apps Script code to link the cloud-based spreadsheet to the web form responses and the document signing system, to automatically update the checklist as each candidate worked their way through the onboarding process, and to pre-populate contract and assignment details based on the candidate's details and specifications for each different job role. After some to and fro, refining the prompts to ChatGPT, they were left with a highly automated system, which automatically tracked the candidate's journey from the initial call and email, clearly providing a visible reference for all candidates in progress and generating all the compliance documents and job role details for a candidate once their start date had been confirmed.

The added benefit is that the automated system is running all the time, so applicants who complete one part of the process will receive an automated email with the next step of the process and they are guided through the registration process even if they complete the registration overnight or at the weekends. Consequently, Workerbee has onboarded more applicants since the system was adopted and has drastically reduced the amount of admin time (by around 400 hours per year at the time of implementation), with the system being fully scalable and adaptable as the business continues to grow.

People

The people lever is often the hardest to tackle quickly but is, nevertheless, vitally important. The starting point here is to consider whether there are any remove me people in the organization and take steps to move them out or, to coin a phrase, 'make them available to the market'. This single step can be sufficient to resolve significant people-related productivity issues.

Case study: Software development consultancy

A team leader in a software development company identified the need for cover during their maternity leave. They recruited another team member, who arrived a few weeks before the maternity leave started. The recruitment process included an initial telephone interview, a face-to-face interview, a psychometric test and an informal 'chat' with the rest of the team. Despite what they thought was a thorough selection process, they got it wrong; once the new recruit started, the atmosphere in the company changed.

This new team member seemed to present one persona when the manager was in the office and a different one when they were not. With the impending maternity leave, this was clearly a concern and, sadly, no matter how good the new person's technical skills might have been, they needed to be removed. As soon as that was done, the manager was approached by each of the remaining team members to thank them, highlighting that this one person was pulling the entire team down.

The next step is supporting those who are leave me and train me with additional training and growth opportunities. This need not be expensive. One of my clients instigated weekly lunch and learn sessions, whereby all staff were invited to attend a lunchtime session in which a colleague shared something they had recently learned or something they thought others might find interesting. Sometimes staff brought their lunch and other times the company provided the lunch. It proved an effective way to offer a peer-to-peer training and development programme.

Smaller organizations often need help to provide career progression for all those who wish for it. The organization's size can be a limiting factor due to fewer available opportunities. A practical solution to resolve this is to provide cross-functional development opportunities. Conducting an Unblock Audit™ could be considered an example of this. Cross-functional development activities are where a team member is offered the opportunity to help with a project outside their department or across the organization as a whole. This can help team members build their own internal support and development networks, aid them in learning new skills and learn more about the organization, helping them stay engaged with an organization.

Prioritization

Identifying priorities

An Unblock Audit™ will generate a long list of possible things to resolve, wishes to grant, challenges to overcome. A common cause of inertia can be where to start first. You do not know where to begin when faced with too many options. I know that when I go to a restaurant with a menu with too many options it can be challenging to choose what to eat. Over time, I have developed a strategy that works well for me. I read the menu, and as soon as I find something I would enjoy, I stop there and select that. I have heard there is science behind menu layout, and restaurants present their most profitable dishes first, so I am probably helping them out; however, it helps me choose quickly and not be overwhelmed by too many options.

There are, though, better strategies to select the best place to start from the many items that have been identified. Sure, it might get you started, and the popular ones might get done first. However, that is not necessarily going to generate the most productivity or be the best strategic decision.

Productivity priority matrix

My approach is to use a simple two-by-two matrix, such as the productivity priority matrix shown below in Figure 8.[72] On one axis we have ease of implementation (effort), which ranges from easy to difficult; on the other, productivity improvement (impact) from low to high.

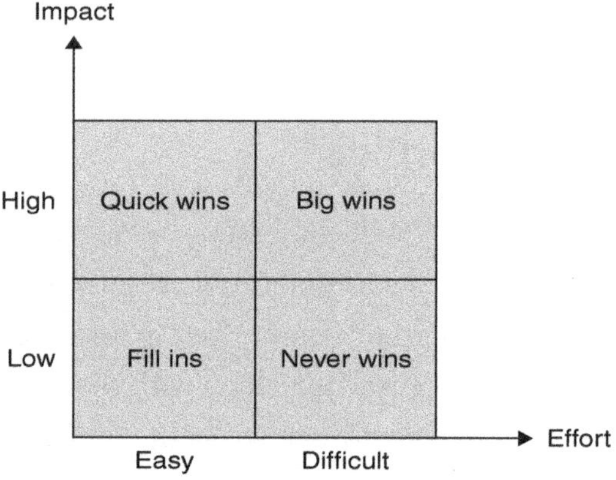

Figure 8 Productivity priority matrix

From the data we have collected during the Unblock Audit™, we should be able to quantify, at least at some level, the productivity improvement for each item on the list. This might be expressed as a time-saving in minutes per day, week or month. It might be described as a cost-saving in £ or defined as a people-saving (i.e. a number of people that can be allocated to other tasks). Using the maximum and minimum ranges we can then allocate those along the y axis.

We then need to ascertain the effort involved in making each productivity change. Again, these can be ranked, perhaps on

72 (Eisenhower 1954)

a scale of 1–10 where those that are in the 1–5 range equate to 'low' and those in the 5–10 range equate to 'high'.

Each item on the list is then mapped to the matrix. If it generates a low productivity gain (e.g. a few minutes a year) and is challenging to implement, it would go in the 'never wins' box. In contrast, if it generates a high productivity gain and is easy to implement, it would go into the quick wins. Mapping these as accurately as possible can help to prioritize within the boxes.

It will not come as any surprise to learn that the starting point is to focus on items in the box that are easy to implement and yield high productivity. I call these *quick wins*.

Big wins involve high productivity gains and are challenging to implement. Often, these must be broken down into smaller projects to ensure they are correctly implemented. The temptation can be to try to do too many of these simultaneously. It is often better to plan them sequentially. Improving productivity is not a one-time thing; it can take multiple years to realize the full potential.

The *fill-ins* are often small projects that can be implemented during a lull, when other tasks are on hold or when waiting for budget approval. The *never wins* are generally not a good use of time, as the effort to implement them outweighs their benefits.

Timing

Understanding where you are on the productivity culture curve can also help you prioritize your action list. If, for example, you are at traumatic, you will need to be looking at different activities to those for organizations that are at problematic, systematic or automatic.

Traumatic

The focus here is on stabilizing operations. The tasks that you should focus on will be aimed at improving cash flow and stabilizing the team. Traumatic indicates a crisis has happened or is happening, so it does not make sense to plunge into lengthy and people-intensive big-win projects at this stage.

Ideas that might be relevant to address first include:

- Quick wins that focus on eliminating unnecessary steps from processes and without the need to reprogram any software.
- Changes to accelerate or improve cash collection which might include changing the timing of invoicing, making direct debit available or providing a frictionless method for customers to make payments.
- Providing checklists as a reference point for staff where there are significant inconsistencies causing problems.
- Recruiting temporary staff to fill a sudden loss of staff (if that is relevant).
- Activities that will help team members feel valued and optimistic, provided this does not conflict with their ability to achieve business objectives.
- Reviewing business objectives to see whether they are still realistic given the current situation; check or pause if appropriate.

Problematic

At problematic, business operations are most likely running along relatively well. Yes, there are problems, and who does not have some of those? It may feel like nothing is broken, meaning the list of things to be tackled can seem overwhelming. However, the focus at problematic is to look at quality.

Quality issues are frequently accepted as a cost of doing business. By quality issues, I mean any of the following:

- Rework – having to redo a job, reprocess a part of a product assembly or repair something that has been returned due to being faulty.
- Revisit – needing to revisit a customer's site to correct or complete work that was not done on the first visit.
- Refund – providing a customer with a refund due to failure to deliver, delivering the wrong thing, a goodwill gesture or an incorrect invoice.
- Replace – sending a replacement due to shipping the wrong product, a faulty product or the product getting broken in transit.

It is helpful to capture metrics around these quality issues. Using the OIR, we can track a holistic metric that outlines our quality. Each adverse quality event counts for 1. The total of all events is then divided by the total number of sales transactions. This can generate a number greater than 100%. For example, if there are three different quality issues on one order, that would be 3/1 (i.e. an OIR of 300%). This might happen, for example, if you ship the wrong goods, so you need to replace them (1), this requires a second delivery to the customer (2), and the delivery driver fails to read the delivery instructions, so when they think they are not home they do not leave it in the safe place, needing to revisit the following day (3).

The OIR percentage you are aiming for is in single digits – 5% is a good number. However, any single-digit number means you are moving out of problematic. When looking at the list of ideas that the Unblock Audit™ has generated, you might want to consider ideas that fit into the following broad themes:

- Adding additional fields to data capture forms to prevent having to go back to a customer to gather additional information.
- Making processes more visible so that where many people are involved, any previous steps that have not been completed are visible.
- Training to help spread good practice among the team – tip of the day sharing at team meetings, or lunch and learn sessions.
- Looking for intelligent ways to prevent rework – for example, audio recording to replace note-taking, and transcription to convert notes to editable text automatically.
- Streamlining processes to ensure that each tool, system or step of the process is only used once, and customers or team members do not need to revisit the same thing multiple times.
- Pre-populating forms and data collection via mail merge tools to reduce the rework by team members and customers.

- Reducing work-in-progress to prevent accidental damage to physical goods or the need to refamiliarize knowledge workers.
- Standardizing all formal customer communications to prevent individual team members having to reinvent wheels.
- Reviewing the quality of any lead generation tools to ensure the reward is worth the effort.
- Removing or streamlining any internal chasing activity – build in structured updates so they become part of the process.
- Creating consistency within all operations to reduce the potential for quality issues.

Systematic

In a systematic culture, many problems have been eradicated through a systematic process of looking at what is happening and then resolving it. The focus at systematic is around capacity, ensuring that an organization is utilizing its existing capacity optimally. If it has not already been done, establishing the capacity constraint within the business is a good starting point. In his award-winning book *The Goal*, Eliyahu M. Goldratt outlines how an organization used the theory of constraints to identify the limiting constraint within the business and made all the other processes subservient.[73]

Failing to understand this concept can result in organizations having constantly conflicting objectives. For example, in *The Goal*, team members identified two bottlenecks in the

---

73 (Goldratt and Cox 2004)

manufacturing operations. Having identified the constraint, the team then looked at how it could create additional capacity and discovered a second outdated machine that it could use for free to increase the capacity of one of the machines, removing it as a constraint. The team also revised processes around the heat treat, identified as the other constraint causing massive delays. Some products were being heat treated multiple times rather than just once or not at all. Everything else worked well by ensuring the constraint operated at total capacity, provided other processes were adjusted to perform at the same rate.

I have worked with clients who have asked me to help them increase their productivity as they see their workers operating at less than full capacity. However, it is not always the right solution to have everyone or every machine running at full capacity. Machines and those who operate them need to be calibrated to perform at the same speed as the constraint within the system. This means that orders flow through continuously, with very little work-in-progress sitting around between processes.

If an early process runs faster than the later constraint, work will build up and be left lying around, prone to spoiling and damage, and, quite frankly, it gets in the way, requiring more space for production operations.

The same is true for service businesses. In a service business, the constraint is most often the number of available billable hours. If the sales team sells these hours faster than the capacity, the lead times to deliver the services will become longer and longer. Sales would need to reduce the rate at which they sell, calibrating their activities to the available capacity, or the capacity needs to be increased. Of course, one way to reduce sales can be to raise prices, although, as we have previously seen, this is not always guaranteed to have the desired effect.

At systematic, we might be looking at activities that meet the following criteria:

- Communicating changes well in advance so all team members know what is coming and understand what will change, why, when, and what is required of them after the change.
- Calibrating sales activities to use the constraint as effectively as possible. For example, if we have excess capacity in the probate team, let's focus our sales activity on that area for a while. If we have too much work for a specific process or machine, what can we sell that uses surplus capacity in other areas of the business and does not require that machine?
- Implementing more extensive software solutions that will start to facilitate automating processes or streamlining information flows around the organization – saving team members' time.
- Creating templates and using conditional formatting of reports to eradicate the need for manual processing of data.
- Joining IT systems together so information passes from one to another without the need for manual intervention.
- Using workflow to create small automations for critical processes to eliminate the need for team members to operate simple workflows manually.

Automatic

An organization with an automatic productivity culture is already well on its way to eliminating unnecessary steps in the process and implementing automation where appropriate. It would typically have established its capacity and worked to utilize it as much as possible. The focus at this point is on throughput. How much volume can the organization put through its capacity, and how can it increase its capacity from there? For example, a facility that can process 1,000 units a month may have finally achieved this objective by completing all the previous suggestions. How can it focus on throughput if it operates at 1,000 units a month? Clearly, if there is a capacity of 1,000 units a month, the organization needs to sell 1,000 units a month. Then it needs to think about how it can expand to more than 1,000 units a month.

Expanding capacity is best tackled when maximum productivity is generated from the existing capacity. At this stage, options may exist to achieve even more out of the current capacity before increasing it.

From a production point of view, automatic might involve replacing outdated equipment with up-to-date machines, particularly robots or equipment that need fewer people to operate. In service industries this might include ML for critical processes.

If we think about the concept of an automatic pilot in a plane, we can see how automatic might be a benefit and how much effort is invested behind the scenes to achieve this. Automatic is not about being robotic and without thought, doing things like an automaton without question; it is more about carefully engineering all the systems and processes so that things run automatically, even when things go wrong.

In an organization with an automatic culture, habits are productive rather than lethargic. Staff demonstrate independent thought and can start, operate or move for the organization's good without having to keep checking in with someone else.

Organizations that have achieved an automatic culture have developed processes to deal with unexpected events, improve current working practices, ensure these changes are effectively communicated and, consequently, ensure that unforeseen events cause minimum disruption.

For organizations that really have fine-tuned their engine and maximized the throughput for their available capacity, the next step is to look at how to increase capacity. For many this might involve opening in another geographical area, putting on another shift in a production line or simply expanding the number of people able to deliver the service.

Activities we might consider at automatic include:

- Developing a process for changing the process.
- Fine-tuning the calibration between sales and capacity to reach optimum throughput.
- Expanding operations through increased capacity.
- Adding value to existing products and services that warrant a higher sales price without significant additional processing.

Change Management

Implementing change

As we have already discussed, the only way to increase an organization's productivity is to change how it functions. As those of us who have been in business for a while are fully aware, change is one of the most challenging things to deliver well.

History is littered with stories of organizations that failed to change and adapt to a new world, even when significant threats loomed on the horizon. And if people cannot change, it is even harder to do it when there is no impetus.

Case study: Blockbuster Video

Blockbuster Video was formed in 1985 in Dallas, Texas, and provided customers with a way to watch movies that had left the cinemas without having to purchase the VHS tape. Using a modern computerized check-out process, Blockbuster offered a vast selection of titles compared to other smaller rental stores. By 1988, Blockbuster was the leading video store chain in the US, with around 800 stores. Overseas expansion saw it move into the UK market in 1992, and in 1994, with over 6,000 stores globally, it was acquired by Viacom for $8.4 billion.

In 1997, Netflix was born, the creation of a Blockbuster customer who was frustrated about the late fees he was charged for returning the VHS tapes late. Blockbuster made 16% of its revenue in late payments, whereas Netflix had no late fees and would send DVDs straight to your house at a fixed monthly cost. Blockbuster failed to sense the change in the market, with customers increasingly becoming disenfranchised by late fees. In 2000, when Blockbuster considered purchasing Netflix for $50 million and decided not to proceed, it was the first step in its eventual demise. Blockbuster eventually launched Blockbuster Online in 2004 and only then decided to end its late fee charging model – a decision estimated to cost $200 million; however, it was already years behind Netflix, and in 2010 Blockbuster filed for bankruptcy.

The gift of Covid

There is no doubt that the Covid-19 pandemic had a significant impact on many organizations. I had clients that put 80% of their staff on furlough, many local businesses closed their doors and struggled to reopen, including my favourite local coffee shop Caffè Nero, and so many felt the personal impact of lockdowns, social isolation and losing loved ones to the virus.

Nevertheless, for many organizations the global Covid-19 pandemic in 2020 was a gift. It created an external impetus to change the way we work that few could argue with. With governments locking down their citizens, restricting movement and preventing 'business as usual', every organization had to rethink how it worked.

I have spoken with people from all walks of life who share a positive Covid story. From my friend who works in the NHS as an occupational therapist, who disclosed that they had been wanting to change shift patterns for years and due to Covid were able to push things through that they would never have otherwise achieved, to the trademark lawyer who shared that by working from home their productivity increased by over 10%.

A friend of mine who worked for a large pharmaceutical company in Belgium was caught high and dry when he travelled to Finland for the weekend to stay with his girlfriend and then found himself unable to return home for many months due to the lockdowns put in place. Working remotely throughout this time helped him justify to his employer that he no longer needed to be in the office and, consequently, no longer needed to live in Belgium. Within two years of the pandemic's start, he sold his house, moved to Finland and married. This would have taken far longer, and he probably would have needed to resign if it had not been for Covid.

The local waste disposal introduced a booking system for when you wanted to go to tip rubbish; the system is still in place, and despite at first glance feeling like a hassle, there is always availability, and we no longer have to queue for ages like we used to do when we picked the same day as everyone else to visit.

The local phlebotomy service had been trying to implement a booking system for years. Without this, different GP practices were allocated specific days of the week, and there was always a massive queue at 9:00 when they opened. Patients would take a ticket on arrival and wait their turn, often waiting for up to an hour as the phlebotomists tried to cram 80% of their daily patients into the first part of the day and then sit twiddling their thumbs for the rest of the morning. During Covid, they finally managed to organize that the GPs would make a booking, spreading the workload throughout the day and avoiding long queues of people.

Creating a sense of urgency

In their best-selling book, *Our Iceberg is Melting*, Kotter and Rathgeber outline the first step in change management as being the need to create a sense of urgency.[74] In their story about penguins living on an iceberg, the sense of urgency they create is an experiment that backs up the findings of one of the penguins and demonstrates that the melting iceberg is at risk of breaking up. Without this life-threatening event hanging over their heads, it would have been almost impossible to achieve what they went on to achieve.

---

[74] (Kotter and Rathgeber 2006)

In any change project, we fight against lethargy – our innate human predisposition to take the easy route in any situation. If we can conserve energy, most of us will choose to do so. Whether it is taking the time to reprogram your fingerprint biometrics on your phone when they unexpectedly cease to function or mending a small hole before it becomes more prominent, we are generally prone to putting things off until a later day. The adage 'a stitch in time saves nine' is entirely relevant in many instances throughout our organizations. Yet we all too often opt for the easiest 'now' solution instead of the route that means we take longer now.

I have a favourite saying: 'Slow down to go faster'. This seemingly paradoxical statement describes how taking the time to slow down, working out how to approach things in the best possible manner, and setting them up to be automated or easily replicated now will ensure that we can go faster in the future. It describes how taking account of all the constituent parts is necessary before taking action. I thought it was a phrase I had coined until I started researching this book and discovered a list of other people using the same or similar words in the same or different contexts.

Ralph Simone did a TEDxUtica presentation titled 'Slow Down to Go Faster: The Power of Pause' in 2017.[75] In it, he references martial arts expert Chuck Norris's 1998 book *Secret Power Within*.[76] He explains how, when Bruce Lee was unable to deal with any of Norris's kicks, he said, 'You're going too fast, your timing is off – you need to slow it down. Slow down to go faster.'

75 (Simone 2017)

76 (Norris 1998)

In *The Fifth Discipline: The Art and Practice of the Learning Organization*, first published in 1990, Peter Senge focuses on group problem-solving using the systems thinking method to convert companies into learning organizations.[77] He writes:

> *'In the long run, the only sustainable competitive advantage is your organization's ability to learn faster than its competitors.' In the quest to build a learning organization, he espouses 11 laws, one of which is 'faster is slower'.*

While this concept applies in many contexts, it can help us spend time setting the scene before we run headlong into the activity phase of improving our productivity. I am reminded of it every time I am able to send long emails at the press of a button – my time investment in creating the templates up front was well worth the effort, and now I am reaping the dividends.

90-day projects

I have been a Vistage member on and off for almost two decades, and one of the most valuable lessons I have learned from the Vistage network is the concept of quarterly projects.[78] I first encountered the concept of quarterly priorities management in Kraig Kramers' *CEO Tools*, a book that was gifted to me by Vistage upon my joining back in 2005.[79] In it, Kramers lists the concept of managing quarterly priorities as one of his critical tools for success.

---

[77] (Senge 1990)

[78] (Vistage, n.d.)

[79] (Kramers 2002)

They also became my focus when I joined the Thought Leader's Business School, which operates a quarterly cycle focused on 90-day projects as a cadence to develop, test and accept or reject new business ideas.

These 90-day projects are a fabulous way to increase productivity, as 90 days is long enough to identify, analyse and implement a productivity change, while being sufficiently short to garner sustained focus from the responsible team.

I have worked with multiple finance teams to implement continuous flow concepts to speed up transaction processing, increase variety, develop capability in finance team members and free up time for business partnering; 90-day projects work perfectly in this environment. The first month is spent understanding the project, defining the changes to be made and communicating them with the relevant stakeholders. Month two is when the new process gets tried out for the first time, and month three is when it is repeated and embedded as a new process. The key is to ensure the project's scope is small enough to deliver in 90 days.

When we work with 90-day projects, we can achieve significant productivity improvements in small chunks. As the famous saying goes, it is best to eat an elephant one bite at a time, and with organizational productivity the same is true. Take it step by step and invest the time in small chunks to crucial business processes.

With 90-day projects, everyone has an opportunity to have a break between initiatives. Whether that is a month before we start the next one, or every 90 days, it is a different team implementing something. The key is ensuring sufficient downtime between projects before the next one starts. It is worth remembering the concept of 'slow down to go faster' again here. There may be a temptation to run multiple consecutive 90-day projects. However, this will likely exhaust the team and is no better than a year-long project, which becomes overwhelming and exhausting.

Make progress visible

We are, as humans, innately focused on what lies ahead, and particularly bad when it comes to acknowledging how far we have come. I recently read a novel where three women and their children fled from terror by swimming across a five-mile channel from one island to another, with only pool floats to aid them.[80] The children included a baby, and in addition they carried an injured man. The water they swam in held the risk of sharks and jellyfish. The story's heroine focuses on looking forwards rather than backwards for the first part of the journey. Swimming was difficult; they were scared, and the children were crying. She knew that if she looked back they might give up, as the danger from which they were fleeing was still so close behind them. However, by the time they had been swimming for a while, and with the horizon seeming so far away, she started to look back and, with relief, could see how far they had come.

There is a lesson here for all of us. When a goal feels far away, we may never feel like we are quite making it. However, along the way, we achieve many successes that we often forget

[80] (Craig 2023)

or belittle, and it can be helpful to capture and regularly acknowledge them.

When I work with organizations, I encourage them to create a real or virtual progress wall. A reminder is added to the wall each day, week or month or upon completion of a tiny target. This could be as simple as a Post-it note or a visual image; for example, a photo. This way, every small thing that is achieved lives for all to see, and as the wall becomes more and more cluttered, the fact that the result still feels a long way off feels less disheartening because everyone can take satisfaction from the visible progress on the progress wall.

Visual stories help change

When our youngest son was seven years old, he was diagnosed as autistic. What followed was a crash course in understanding autism and how we could best support him in navigating a non-autistic world. One of the key lessons we learned was the power of visual stories. Autistic people, particularly children, can struggle to give meaning to language. They may understand the words and often have trouble understanding the meaning. We discovered this was entirely true for our son.

As we live relatively close to London, we were in the habit of taking day trips there occasionally. We might go to the theatre or visit museums or tourist attractions. Almost every time we were due to go, my son would disappear on the day and hide, as he did not want to leave the house.

After his diagnosis, and having heard about the power of visual stories, we had an experience that changed our lives and approach forever. The Globe Theatre put on a relaxed production of *Othello*, and we were lucky enough to get four tickets. After purchasing the tickets, we were sent a visual story for the event. It was the first time I had seen a visual story, and I was blown away by it. A few days before the trip I sat down with our son and went through it with him. It was a simple and detailed A4 booklet containing photos of what to expect, with some narrative under each. It started with photos of the large gates at the entrance to the Globe Theatre. It showed the courtyard and photos of the staff in their red aprons, explaining that they were there to help. There were photos of the ticket office, explaining that you might need to queue to collect your tickets, and the café/restaurant, noting that other people might also be there. A photo of a chill room – somewhere you can go if you need a break. On it went, anticipating everything that might happen. It also included an overview of the play, complete with when to expect a flashing light or a loud explosion.

On the day of the trip, when we announced it was time to get ready to go, for the first time in his nearly eight years he put on his shoes without a fuss and climbed into the car, excited about the trip ahead.

Since that day we have used visual stories whenever we needed to help him understand something unknown. We still do, even though he is now in his teens. A quick look at the website of a venue we are visiting so he can see what to expect, or a look at Google Street View to show where we are going is enough to help him engage in the trip ahead, reducing anxiety.

These techniques work because they reduce anxiety. Anxiety causes stress, which increases cortisol and can result in the prefrontal cortex shutting down. The prefrontal cortex is the part of the brain we use for rational thought, organization and planning. If that is not working, we rely on our freeze, flight or fight instincts from our amygdala or 'old brain'.

Companies undergoing significant change unwittingly put their team members into a similar situation. Most of the conversations about the change project are undertaken in meetings, town halls or through written emails and newsletters. Change is all about the unknown, and this causes anxiety and stress, albeit at different levels, in our team members. Some will manage the stress easily and enjoy the experience; for many the fear of the unknown will create sufficient stress that they may be unable to embrace it in the way you wish. Most often, the response is that they freeze, and in so doing resist the change and try to carry on working the same way. Or they flee, sometimes by leaving the organization. Few choose to fight, and those who do become vocal opponents of the changes, infecting others with their stress.

This is another place where we need to slow down to go faster. If we treat all team members as if they are metaphorically autistic and create powerful visual stories for the forthcoming change, it will make that change more manageable and faster in the long run.

The human brain first thought in pictures. Our ancestors used the land to navigate and drew images of the animals they hunted on the inside of caves. Language is a relatively new invention in evolution, so when our old brain kicks in it is no real surprise that visuals are the best way to cut through and be heard.

What does this mean in practice? The potential solution will vary according to the situation. A significant office move can be made more accessible by providing staff with a plan of the new environment, showing where they will be sitting, and 3D visualizations of the space. Can you help them 'sit' in their new environment and show them what they will see? Can you show them the new kitchen area and the bathrooms, where they will store their belongings (if moving to an open-plan environment)? Make it as accurate and as visual as you can.

If you are physically moving to a new building, different issues may arise. How will my journey change? Where will I store my bike or park my car? By creating a visual story of how to do these things, team members will be reassured that everything has been thought about, and there will be little disruption to their daily lives.

If implementing new processes or software, flow diagrams help; however, there is something less visceral about a flow diagram compared to photos of the different processes or mock-ups of a new screen.

Of course, my suggestion here is that you treat your team members as if they metaphorically are autistic. And you might have some #actuallyAutistic team members as well.

If that is the case, or you have team members with other neurodiversities, these suggestions are even more critical and almost certainly not optional. If you want to navigate this change with your team intact, slow down, create the visuals and over-communicate at every step.

The case for diversity

Diversity has an important role to play in improving productivity. While the diversity, equity and inclusion agenda has historically focused on gender and racial or ethnic diversity, there is a case to be made for casting the net wider and including age, geography and neurodiversity within its scope. A McKinsey study, 'Diversity Matters', of 366 public companies across a range of industries in the UK, the US, Latin America and Canada found:

> *'Companies in the top quartile for racial and ethnic diversity are 35 per cent more likely to have financial returns above their respective national industry medians.'*

and

> *'Companies in the top quartile for gender diversity are 15 per cent more likely to have financial returns above their respective national industry medians.'*[81]

Meanwhile, research indicates that some teams with neurodivergent team members may be up to 30% more productive than those without them.[82]

---

[81] (Hunt, Layton and Prince 2015)

[82] (Austin and Pisano 2017)

A further study in which pairs were tasked with building a tower from dried spaghetti and plasticine found the least similarity in designs from neurodiverse pairs (one autistic person and one non-autistic person) compared to single-neurotype pairs (either two autistic people with a similar diagnosis or two non-autistic people).[83]

These studies indicate that creating diverse and inclusive workplaces has significant business benefits in addition to its social benefits. More diverse organizations are better able to challenge the status quo, innovate and deliver improved business outcomes than their less diverse competitors.

A 2010 article 'The Decision-Driven Organization' by Bain & Co., published in *Harvard Business Review* asserts that:

> *'Ultimately, a company's value is just the sum of the decisions it makes and executes.'*[84]

If this assertion is true, we can argue that a company's productivity is affected by the sum of its decisions and execution. Therefore, we must improve our organization's decision-making to become more productive.

The Bain & Co. article outlines the benefits of conducting a decision audit to understand the decisions that are critical to delivering successfully on a company's strategy. Armed with this information, the next step is to determine the level within the organization at which those decisions must be made and executed to deliver the most value.

---

83 (Axbey, et al. 2023)

84 (Blenko, Mankins and Rogers 2010)

Nevertheless, even with a decision-driven organization, the quality of our decisions may not be optimum if we lack diversity within our organizations. This topic is of increasing interest to researchers, and their findings are fascinating. While we often feel that the decisions we make within homogenous groups may be better, the reality is that when everyone agrees with each other, the quality of our decision-making is sub-optimal. The decision-making feels easier; however, in practice, dissenting views that challenge others enhance team performance.

For example, a study conducted by Cloverpop and reported in Forbes.com found:

- Inclusive teams make better business decisions up to 87% of the time.
- Teams that follow an inclusive process make decisions twice as fast and with half the meetings.
- Decisions made and executed by diverse teams delivered 60% better results.[85]

Reasons cited for diverse teams making better decisions include:

- Focus on facts; there may be more scrutiny of each other's actions. There is a lower risk of group think, which may lead to overlooking key pieces of information.
- Process more carefully; there may be more careful consideration of the perspectives of people who think differently than they do.

---

85 (Larson 2017)

- More innovative; conformity works against innovative thinking; diverse perspectives encourage different thinking around existing problems.[86]

In conclusion, when considering how best to tackle change management for your productivity improvement programme, think carefully about the diversity of your organization and, importantly, the diversity of your decision-making. Look for ways to increase diversity across as many aspects as you can: race, gender, age, geography and neurodiversity.

Case study: Neurodiverse problem-solving

We visited the Ironbridge museums in Telford on a family holiday to Shropshire. One of the museums is Enginuity, an interactive museum focused on engineering.[87] It comprises a wide range of exhibits, many of which are hands-on. You can learn how a blast furnace works, understand how water power is used and learn about the first electric car made in the area. One of the tabletop activities is to build an arch from pieces of wood that replicate the stones. My husband, a civil engineer, and our eldest son spent a long time playing with the various pieces, trying to get the keystone into place so it would hold everything

[86] (Rock and Grant 2016)

[87] (Ironbridge, n.d.)

else up and, despite their attempts and combined knowledge, failed spectacularly. Our youngest son, who until this point had been working on a different problem, unable to see their efforts, approached the table and, after a few moments of exploration, picked up the one wooden piece that neither my husband nor our elder son had noticed. It was a semi-spherical form, which he put in place, then proceeded to fit all the stones above it and removed the form to leave the arch holding steady. It was all the more entertaining to watch, as he had no idea how long his brother and father had struggled, and the look on their faces as they saw how quickly he solved the problem was priceless. It is an example of how his autistic mind frequently sees things differently from how we see them.

Summary

Your 100-day improvement plan

So, now that you have read the book, I hope it has inspired you to start to look at your organization's productivity culture and think about what it might take to improve it.

Throughout this book, I have examined the four key drivers of productivity: promise, price, process and people. As you will have seen, I have illustrated how each can have different levels of sophistication and, hence, capacity to enhance productivity.

Astute readers may have already realized that these four levers are linked. Our organizations are a system, and no individual driver can stand alone. If the promise side of the pyramid is low down, it is likely to make it harder to ascend higher on the other sides, for example. It is almost as if you need to ascend a layer at a time around the pyramid or pick the most important lever first and start there.

Every organization starts from somewhere different. It will have its unique history, relationships, commercial realities and available resources to bring productivity improvement. For this reason, each organization's recipe is likely to be somewhat different. However, in most cases, the steps laid out below will get you on your way.

1. Measure it – before you start doing anything, measure your productivity and calculate your PWQ. If possible, calculate it retrospectively for the last couple of years or the last four quarters and see in which direction it is moving.
2. Use your PWQ to identify your current productivity culture. Understand the behaviours that typify that culture and work with your leadership team and management hierarchy to validate your findings.
3. Review the four drivers and assess which level of the productivity pyramid you are operating for each. You may find you have multiple answers for some sides; for example, the promise side may apply to your organization as a whole. However, the people or process side could have different answers for different departments or processes.
4. Identify your facilitators – at least two people internally or an external facilitator – and conduct an Unblock Audit™ to find all the candidates for change.
5. Review the findings and prioritize them using the productivity priority matrix.
6. Pick one or two of the quick wins and create 90-day projects to deliver change.
7. Build a success wall or board and record progress as you go.

8. Remeasure your productivity every 90 days and ensure your decisions are moving you in the right direction, understanding that productivity may drop slightly if your team is invested in business improvement rather than business development and delivery.

None of this will be an overnight recipe for transformation. Significant improvements in productivity require investment over several years. Remember, we are talking about a cultural transformation; at the heart of that are human beings who resist change. The key is to make a start, embrace the ideas and recognize that underneath all the resistance is lethargy, and that we need to find creative ways to engage our brains to overcome this.

Acknowledgements

In 2019, when I wrote my first book, I established a writing pattern that seems to have worked again. I have discovered that I find it almost impossible to fit writing in among the day-to-day activities of a busy life, and I have to carve out time and completely 'get away from it'. I was inspired to adopt this approach by my friend Bob Cooney, whose approach to writing his book *Real Money from Virtual Reality* in 2018 was to book a voyage on a container ship across the Arctic, where he had no distractions and promised himself a coffee each day only after he had reached his daily word target.

In my case, I did a deal with my husband that I would write 1,500 words a day on each day of our three-week trip around Scotland as we drove the NC500 in our motorhome. As a result, 95% of this book was completed quickly, and it has taken only a few more months, mainly during holidays, to complete the final edit.

The title of this book resulted from a brainstorming session I undertook as part of a skills swap with Rhea Wessel, writer and founder at The Institute for Thought Leaders. I undertook an Unblock Audit™ on her business, and after presenting my findings she helped me shape my rather random thoughts into a coherent proposition. Thank you, Rhea. I hope you enjoy the result.

This book has been many years in the making despite only taking a few weeks to write. It is the culmination of nearly three decades of supporting a range of clients to improve their productivity. During this time I have sometimes struggled to clearly and succinctly articulate my thoughts in a way that others can easily access, and it is in large part down to my former Vistage group and its chair, Chris Hughes, that I have finally got somewhere close. They challenged me to create a model to provide the context for my thinking. That challenge resulted in the early versions of the productivity pyramid.

I fell in love with models, largely thanks to Matt Church and the team at Thought Leaders Business School. This book is supported by several models, which I hope will make the concepts I describe accessible to a wide audience.

While I provide support to a range of organizations on all aspects of the productivity pyramid, my thinking has been heavily influenced by teachings from some amazing practitioners. I would like to thank Bob Gorton for introducing me to the 'critical resource limitation' and the work of Brian Warnes; Chris Hughes for his advice over many years on all things marketing; and Barnaby Wynter, who has helped me understand the way in which organizations can communicate their brand promise. I have learned so much from all of you, and I hope I do justice to what are, without question, your areas of expertise.

Thanks to Beth Hutchins of Just Content for the developmental editing. Everything you picked up was where I knew I had taken shortcuts and wanted it off my desk. I hope I have incorporated all your comments, and I am sure the book is better for it.

To the team at Practical Inspiration Publishing, and in particular Alison Jones, thank you for believing in this concept so quickly and reassuring me that this is a book worthy of publishing.

Finally, and most importantly of all, I need to thank my family. To my husband, Ian, for giving me the space to do my thing without pressure or recrimination when things have not necessarily gone the right way. Over many years you have supported me as and when required, emotionally, financially and practically. And to our two sons, Alex and Felix, whose life journeys as neurodiverse young men, posing questions about life, learning and what Mum does for a living have kept us all entertained.

Bibliography

Austin, Robert D., and Gary P. Pisano. 2017. 'Neurodiversity as a Competitive Advantage.' *Harvard Business Review* 96–103. Accessed 9 April 2024. https://hbr.org/2017/05/neurodiversity-as-a-competitive-advantage

Axbey, Harriet, Nadin Beckmann, Sue Fletcher-Watson, Alisdair Tullo, and Catherine J. Crompton. 2023. 'Innovation Through Neurodiversity: Diversity is Beneficial.' *Sage Journals: Autism* 27 (7): 2193–2198. doi:10.1177/1362361323115868

Be The Business. n.d. *Be The Business.* Accessed 9 April 2024. www.bethebusiness.com/

Blenko, Marcia W., Michael Mankins, and Paul Rogers. 2010. 'The Decision-Driven Organization.' *Harvard Business Review*, June. Accessed 9 April 2024. https://hbr.org/2010/06/the-decision-driven-organization

Boisgontier, Matthieu P., Boris Cheval, Eda Tipura, Nicholas Burra, Jaromil Frossard, Julien Chanal, Dan Orsholits, and Rémi Radel. 2018. 'Avoiding Sedentary Behaviors Requires More Cortical Resources than Avoiding Physical Activity: An EEG Study.' *Neuropsychologia* 119: 68–80. doi:10.1016/j.neuropsychologia.2018.07.029

Brown, Polly S., and John D. Gould. 1987. 'An Experimental Study of People Creating.' *ACM Transactions on Office Information Systems*, (IBM Thomas J. Watson Research Center) 5: 258–272. doi:10.1145/27641.28058

Buckingham, Marcus, and Curt Coffman. 1999. *First Break All the Rules.* The Gallup Organization.

Carnegie, Dale. 2018. *How to Win Friends and Influence People.* Jaico Publishing House.

Chartered Management Institute. 2023. 'Taking Responsibility: Why UK Plc Needs Better Managers.' *managers.org.uk.* October. Accessed 9 April 2024. www.managers.org.uk/wp-content/uploads/2023/10/CMI_BMB_GoodManagment_Report.pdf

Collegiat Strength & Condidtioning Coaches Association (CSCCA). 2012. *Baseball Great Releases e-Book.* 27 September. Accessed 9 April 2024. www.cscca.org/news/newsroom?job=detail&id=44

Collins, Jim. 2001. *Good to Great.* Collins Business.

—. 2009. *How the Mighty Fall.* Random House Business.

Collins, Jim, and Morten T. Hansen. 2011. *Great by Choice: Uncertainty, Chaos and Luck – Why Some Thrive Despite Them All.* New York: Harper Collins Publishers.

Craig, Holly. 2023. *The Shallows.* Thomas & Mercer.

Crystal Ski. 2023/24. *Snow Promise.* Accessed 9 April 2024. www.crystalski.co.uk/ski-holidays/the-crystal-snow-promise

n.d. *David Hall.* Accessed 9 April 2024. www.linkedin.com/in/david-hall-458b37/

Davis, Hunter. 1993. *INTERVIEW / How Gerald was well and truly ratnered.* 2 November. Accessed 9 April 2024. www.independent.co.uk/life-style/interview-how-gerald-was-well-and-truly-ratnered-what-does-a-man-do-when-he-s-made-the-most-expensive-crack-in-history-well-he-learns-a-lot-of-things-he-never-knew-before-1501608.html

de Ternay, Guerric. 2024. *Apple Value Proposition In a Nutshell.* 5 February. Accessed 9 April 2024. https://fourweekmba.com/apple-value-proposition

Department for Education. 2023. *Employer Skills Survey 2022.* 28 September. Accessed 9 April 2024. https://explore-education-statistics.service.gov.uk/find-statistics/employer-skills-survey/2022

Edmondson, Amy C. 2018. *The Fearless Organization: Creating Psychological Safety in the Workplace for Learning, Innovation, and Growth.* Wiley.

Eisenhower, Dwight D. 1954. *Adapted from Task Priority Matrices, variations on the original urgent / important priority matrix the Eisenhower Matrix*. Evanston, August 19. www.presidency.ucsb.edu/documents/address-the-second-assembly-the-world-council-churches-evanston-illinois

Expert Panel, Forbes Technology Council. 2019. '5 Smart Ways Machine Learning Helps Businesses and Entrepreneurs.' *Forbes.com*. 11 September. Accessed 9 April 2024. www.forbes.com/sites/forbestechcouncil/2019/09/11/15-smart-ways-machine-learning-helps-businesses-and-entrepreneurs/?sh=3799eea27f67

Fairlie, Mark. 2023. 'How Machine Learning Is Boosting Business Growth.' *Business.com*. 3 November Accessed 9 April 2024. www.business.com/articles/machine-learning-boosts-business-growth/

Francis-Devine, Brigid, and Andrew Powell. 2024. *UK Labour Market Statistics*. House of Commons Library, 17. Accessed 9 April 2024, https://researchbriefings.files.parliament.uk/documents/CBP-9366/CBP-9366.pdf

Gallup. 2017. *State of the Global Workplace*. Gallup, 5, 37.

Gallup. 2024. *State of the Global Workplace*. Gallup, 30. Accessed 9 April 2024. https://www.gallup.com/workplace/349484/state-of-the-global-workplace.aspx

Goldratt, Eliyahu M., and Jeff Cox. 2004. *The Goal: A Process of Ongoing Improvement*. Abingdon & New York: Gower Publishing.

Gorton, Bob. 2007. *Boosting Sales: Increasing Profits Without Breaking the Bank*. London: A. C. Black.

Hamel, Gary. 2009. *What Really Kills Great Companies: Inertia*. 29 September. Accessed 9 April 2024. www.wsj.com/articles/BL-GHMB-125

Heskett, James L., W. Earl Sasser Jr., and Leonard A. Schlesinger. 1997. *The Service Profit Chain: How Leading Companies Link Profit and Growth to Loyalty, Satisfaction, and Value*. Free Press.

Hill, Napoleon. 1939. *Think and Grow Rich: Teaching, for the First Time, the Famous Andrew Carnegie Formula for Money-making, Based Upon the Thirteen Proven Steps to Riches*. Ralston Society.

Hunt, Vivian, Dennis Layton, and Sara Prince. 2015. 'Diversity Matters.' McKinsey & Company. Accessed 9 April 2024. www.mckinsey.com/insights/organization/~/media/2497d4ae4b534ee89d929cc6e3aea485.ashx

Hunt-Davis, Ben, and Harriet Beveridge. 2011. *Will it Make the Boat Go Faster? Olympic-Winning Strategies for Everyday Success*. Matador.

InMoment. 2018. '2018 Retail CX Trends Report: Trust and Loyalty in the Experience Economy.' 10. Accessed 9 April 2024. https://inmoment.com/resource/2018-retail-cx-trends-report/

Ironbridge. n.d. Enginuity. Accessed 9 April 2024 http://www.ironbridge.org.uk/visit/enginuity/

Kotter, John P. 2012. *Leading Change, with a New Preface by the Author.* Boston: Harvard Business Review Press.

Kotter, John, and Holger Rathgeber. 2006. *Our Iceberg is Melting: Changing and Succeeding Under Any Conditions.* Macmillan.

Kramers, Kraig. 2002. *CEO TOOLS: The Nuts-n-Bolts of Business for Every Manager's Success.* HA&W CEO Tools, LLC.

Larson, Erik. 2017. 'New Research: Diversity + Inclusion = Better Decision Making at Work.' *Forbes.com.* 21 September. Accessed 9 April 2024. www.forbes.com/sites/eriklarson/2017/09/21/new-research-diversity-inclusion-better-decision-making-at-work

Manson, Emily. 2007. 'Jamie Oliver's Dinner Lady Quits Her Job.' *The Caterer.* 4 April. Accessed 9 April 2024. www.thecaterer.com/news/jamie-olivers-dinner-lady-quits-her-job

Martin-Fagg, Roger. n.d. www.linkedin.com/in/rogermartinfagg

Matthews, Sam. 2005. 'Jamie Oliver Triumphs as Government Earmarks £280m for School Dinners.' *Campaign Live.* 30 March. Accessed 9 April 2024. www.campaignlive.co.uk/article/jamie-oliver-triumphs-government-earmarks-280m-school-dinners/468490

Matzler, Kurt, Birgit Renzl, and Andreas Würtele. 2006. 'Dimensions of Price Satisfaction: A Study in the Retail Banking Industry.' *International Journal of Bank Marketing* 24 (4): 221. doi:10.1108/02652320610671324

McKinsey & Co. 2014. *The Three Cs of Customer Satisfaction: Consistency, Consistency, Consistency.* McKinsey & Co. Accessed 9 April 2024. www.mckinsey.com/industries/retail/our-insights/the-three-cs-of-customer-satisfaction-consistency-consistency-consistency#/

McKinsey Global Institute. 2018. 'Solving the United Kingdom's Productivity Puzzle in a Digital Age.' *mckinsey.com.* September. Accessed 9 April 2024. www.mckinsey.com/featured-insights/regions-in-focus/solving-the-united-kingdoms-productivity-puzzle-in-a-digital-age

Middleton, Christopher. 2006. 'Monsterella Pizza the Order of the Day for TV's Unlikeliest Superchef.' *The Telegraph.* 8 April Accessed 9 April 2024. www.telegraph.co.uk/foodanddrink/3325118/Monsterella-pizza-the-order-of-the-day-for-TVs-unlikeliest-superchef.html

Murphy, Mark. 2018. *If Your Employees Aren't Learning, You're Not Leading.* 21 January. Accessed 9 April 2024. www.forbes.com/sites/markmurphy/2018/01/21/if-your-employees-arent-learning-youre-not-leading/

Norris, Chuck. 1998. *Secret Power Within: Zen Solutions to Real Problems.* Bantam Doubleday Dell Publishing Group.

Office for National Statistics (ONS). 2018. *Management Practices and Productivity in British Production and Services Industries: Initial Results from the Management and Expectations Survey: 2016.* 6 April. Accessed 9 April 2024. www.ons.gov.uk/employmentandlabourmarket/peopleinwork/labourproductivity/articles/experimentaldataonthemanagementpracticesofmanufacturingbusinessesingreatbritain/2018-04-06

—. 2024. *Average Weekly Earnings in Great Britain: March 2024.* 12 March. Accessed 9 April 2024. www.ons.gov.uk/employmentandlabourmarket/peopleinwork/employmentandemployeetypes/bulletins/averageweeklyearningsingreatbritain/march2024

—. 2024. *UK Whole Economy: Output per Hour Worked % Change per Annum SA.* 15 February. Accessed 9 April 2024. www.ons.gov.uk/employmentandlabourmarket/peopleinwork/labourproductivity/timeseries/lzvd/prdy

Peale, Norman Vincent. 1989. *The Inspirational Writings.* New York: Inspirational Press.

Plant Planet. 2021. *A Brief History of the Combine Harvester.* 21 August. Accessed 9 April 2024. www.plant-planet.co.uk/a-brief-history-of-the-combine-harvester/

Productivity Leadership Group. 2016. 'How Good is Your Business Really? Raising Our Amibitions for Business Performance.' *Be The Business.* Accessed 9 April 2024. https://bethebusiness.com/our-thinking/how-good-is-your-business-really-raising-our-ambitions-for-business-performance

PwC. 2018. 'Experience is Everything: Here's How to Get it Right.' *pwc.com.* Accessed 9 April 2024. www.pwc.com/us/en/advisory-services/publications/consumer-intelligence-series/pwc-consumer-intelligence-series-customer-experience.pdf#page=8

Ratner, Gerald. 2007. *Gerald Ratner: The Rise and Fall... and Rise Again.* Capstone.

Reichheld, Frederick F., and Phil Schefter. 2000. 'The Economics of E-Loyalty.' *Harvard Business School.* 7 October. Accessed 9 April 2024. https://hbswk.hbs.edu/archive/the-economics-of-e-loyalty

Richer, Julian. 2001. *The Richer Way.* Richer Publishing.

Rock, David, and Heidi Grant. 2016. 'Why Diverse Teams Are Smarter.' *Harvard Business Review.* 4 November. Accessed 9 April 2024. https://hbr.org/2016/11/why-diverse-teams-are-smarter

Sasser, Jr., W. Earl, and Frederick F. Reichheld. 1990. 'Zero Defections: Quality Comes to Services.' *Harvard Business Review*, September–October. Accessed 9 April 2024. https://hbr.org/1990/09/zero-defections-quality-comes-to-services

Schwantes, Marcel. 2019. *Study: 37 Percent of Employees Say They Would Leave Their Current Job Today if They Were Not Offered This 1 Perk.* 25 April. Accessed 9 April 2024. www.inc.com/marcel-schwantes/study-37-percent-of-employees-say-they-would-leave-their-current-job-today-if-they-were-not-offered-this-1-perk.html

Senge, Peter M. 1990. *The Fifth Discipline: The Art and Practice of the Learning Organization.* Second edition April 2006. Random House Business.

Shacknai, Gabby. 2022. *Inside the Success of Dyson Hair – and Its Decision to Redesign the Bestselling Airwrap Tool.* 11 June. Accessed 9 April 2024. www.forbes.com/sites/gabbyshacknai/2022/06/11/inside-the-success-of-dyson-hair-and-its-decision-to-redesign-the-bestselling-airwrap-tool

Sheetz, Steven D., and S. E. Kruck. 2001. 'Spreadsheet Accuracy Theory.' *Journal of Information Systems Education* 12 (2): 93–106.

Simone, Ralph. 2017. *Slow Down to Go Faster: The Power of Pause*. September. Accessed 9 April 2024. www.ted.com/talks/ralph_simone_slow_down_to_go_faster_the_power_of_pause

Society of Estate Clerks of Works. 1908. *The Journal of the Society of Estate Clerks of Works* 21: 30.

Statista Research Department. 2024. *Unemployment Rate in the United States from 1990 to 2022*. 23 February. Accessed 9 April 2024. www.statista.com/statistics/193290/unemployment-rate-in-the-usa-since-1990

Thornhill, Jo, and Laura Howard. 2024. *Average UK Salary By Age In 2024*. 9 April. Accessed 10 April 2024. www.forbes.com/uk/advisor/business/average-uk-salary-by-age/

Vistage. n.d. Homepage. Accessed 9 April 2024 http://www.vistage.co.uk

Warnes, Brian. 1984. *The Genghis Khan Guide to Business*. London: Osmosis Publications.

Which? 2023. '98% of Black Friday "Deals" Aren't the Cheapest Price of the Year.' *which.co.uk*. 21 November. Accessed 9 April 2024. www.which.co.uk/news/article/98-of-black-friday-deals-arent-the-cheapest-price-of-the-year-aey1d9q3h1Bu

Whitehurst, Jim. 2016. *Leaders Can Shape Company Culture Through Their Behaviors*. 13 October. Accessed 9 April 2024.

https://hbr.org/2016/10/leaders-can-shape-company-culture-through-their-behaviors

Wikipedia – UK Recessions. n.d. *List of Recessions in the United Kingdom.* Accessed 9 April 2024. https://en.wikipedia.org/wiki/List_of_recessions_in_the_United_Kingdom

Wikipedia – Dusty Baker. n.d. *Dusty Baker.* Accessed 9 April 2024. https://en.wikipedia.org/wiki/Dusty_Baker

Wikipedia – Jamie's School Dinners. 2012. *Jamie's School Dinners.* Accessed 9 April 2024. https://en.wikipedia.org/wiki/Jamie%27s_School_Dinners

Wiley, Jack. 2023. *Why Management Training Remains Important.* 16 February. Accessed 9 April 2024. https://trainingmag.com/why-management-training-remains-important/

Wynter, Barnaby. 2010. *The Brand Bucket: Make Your Marketing Work.* Cirencester: Management Books 2000 Ltd.

—. n.d. *The Brand Bucket Company.* Accessed 9 April 2024. www.thebrandbucketcompany.com

Zendesk. 2020. 'Zendesk Customer Experience Trends Report 2020.' 6. Accessed 9 April 2024. https://d1eipm3vz40hy0.cloudfront.net/pdf/cxtrends/cx-trends-2020-full-report.pdf

Index

A
Amazon 57
Apple 61–62, 77
artificial intelligence (AI) 131–134, 139
  automate routine tasks 132
  and decision-making 133–134
  leaner manufacturing 133
  and logistics 133
  and personalization 133
  and risk gauging 132
automated processes 123 127, 132, 137–139, 177–179
automatic cultures
  and prioritization 192–193
  of productivity 33–34, 192–193
  soft fruit packing (case study) 34–35

B
Bain & Co. 208
Baker, Dusty 30
Be the Business programme 2
big wins 184, 185, 186
Blockbuster Video 195–196
Blue Rocket accounting 173–174
brand, definition of 47
brand loyalty 57–59
  I know model 60
  known model 61–62
  they know model 61
  we know model 60–61
  who knows? model 59–60
Brand24 139–140
Brandwatch Consumer Intelligence 139
break-even point 65–66, 73

C
Cadbury, mum's birthday advert 102
capacity constraint 189–190
Carnegie, Dale 103
challenge me team members 98–99
  case study 99–100

management of 107–108
change, *see also* new ideas and change
Blockbuster Video (case study) 195–196
and Covid pandemic 196–198
creating a sense of urgency 198–200
and diversity 207–210
implementation 195
making progress visible 202–203
neurodiverse problem-solving (case study) 210–211
90-day projects 200–202
and productivity 13–15
and visual stories 203–207
charities 5–6
ChatGPT 131, 132, 178–179
Cloverpop 209
Collins, Jim 34, 88, 99, 164
competitive pricing 70–71
constraints, theory of 189–190
Covid pandemic 196–198
critical resource limitation (CRL) 72–74, 175
CRM systems, automation of 138
cross-functional development activities 181
Crystal Ski 46
customer value equation 75
customizations 125

D
data analysis 139
data transfers 138–139
decision-making
audit 208–210
automated process in 133
depreciation 42–43
discounted pricing 69–70
disengaged team members 89–92
diversity, and change 207–210
dynamic pricing 71–74
Dyson 55

E
education, and productivity 8–9, 15
ERP (enterprise resource planning) systems 125, 135, 158, 176
explicit processes 119–123, 136–137

F
facilitators 143–144, 163, 214
Fathom 139
fill-ins 184, 185
financial crisis 2008 7
flow diagrams 137
formula, of productivity 43
FTE (full-time equivalent) calculation 4, 42

G
galvanize me team members 100–103
case study 102
management of 108–109
GB rowing team 52
Goldratt, Eliyahu M. 189
goodwill 47
Gorton, Bob 72
gross value added (GVA) 4
group think 164

H
Hall, David 22–23
Hamel, Gary 27
Hill, Napoleon 80
100-day improvement plan 213–215

I
I know model 49–51, 60

inflation 68
intelligent processes 128, 139–140
  AI, *see* artificial intelligence (AI)
  RACI (responsible, accountable, consulted, informed), documenting 129–131
  tools, role of 134–140
investment in technology, and productivity 9–11, 15–16

K
known model 54–56, 61–62
Kotter's change model 95
Kramers, Kraig 200

L
leaner manufacturing, automated process in 133
leave me team members 92–96
  case study 94
  management of 106–107
lethargy 14, 15–16, 21–22, 199, 215
logistics, automated process in 133

M
machine language (ML) 131–133, 139
macroeconomic factors, of productivity 12–13
management practices, and productivity 11–12, 16
marketing automation 123–124
McKinsey & Co. 117–118, 207
mean average salary, and productivity 4–5
MySupermarket 71

N
Netflix 196
net profit 42–43
never wins 185
new ideas and change 161–165; *see also* change
  establishing 161–163
  ideal time for 164–165
  testing 163–164
90-day projects 200–202, 214–215

O
Old St Andrews Whisky 74
online tracking systems 138
order integrity ratio (OIR) 187–188
order to cash (O2C) 146
  mapping 147–148
  overview 146–147
organizational culture 19
overheads 66–67

P
P2P process 166
Peale, Norman Vincent 33
people 87–89, 180–181
  Cadbury, mum's birthday advert (case study) 102
  challenge me category 98–99, 107–108
  Excel train me (case study) 97–98
  galvanize me category 100–103, 108–109
  leave me category 92–96, 106–107
  management of 103–109
  remove me category 89–90, 106
  Sands, Nora (case study) 104–105
  software development consultancy (case study) 180–181
  train me category 94, 96–97, 107

personalization improvement, automated process in 133
phantom price list 70
Polyfilla systems 158
price 63–64, 174–175
  break-even point 65–66, 73
  competitive 70–71, 83
  contrasting flight experiences (case study) 75–76
  discounted 69–70, 82–83
  dynamic 71–74, 84
  going the extra mile 80–81
  housing association (case study) 175
  knowing where to tap (case study) 79
  marketing workshops (case study) 77–78
  overheads 66–67, 72–73
  patent lawyer (case study) 78
  price confidence 81–85
  pricing levels 65
  pricing strategy 64–65
  stagnant 67–69, 82
  valued 75–80, 84–85
  whisky industry (case study) 74
prioritization 183–193
  identification of priorities 183–184
  productivity priority matrix 184–185
  timing 185–193
problematic cultures
  glazing manufacturer (case study) 22
  laboratory (case study) 23–24
  and prioritization 187–189
  of productivity 20–25, 187–189
process 111–112, 176–178
  accountancy firm (case study) 120
  audiovisual company (case study) 121–122
  automated 123–127, 137–139
  blind manufacturer (case study) 118
  building materials (case study) 127–128
  clothing manufacturer (case study) 125
  explicit 119–123, 136–137
  hockey club (case study) 114–115
  intelligent 128, 139–140
  kitchen manufacturer (case study) 177
  manufacturer (case study) 126–127
  prioritization, *see* prioritization
  prototyped 112–115, 135, 125
  tacit 115–118, 135–136, 125
  Workerbee recruitment (case study) 178–179
productivity
  and change 13–15
  and charities 5–6
  decrease in 6–7
  and education 8–9, 15
  growth, calculation of 5
  and lack of investment in technology 9–11, 15–16
  and lethargy 14, 15–16
  macroeconomic factors 12–13
  and management practices 11–12, 16
  meaning of 3–6
  puzzle 1–2
  root cause of issues 7–15
  and skills gap 8–9, 15
productivity cultures 17–19
  automatic 33–34
  overall culture 35
  problematic 20–25
  systematic 29–32
  traumatic 25–28
productivity drivers 41–44

depreciation 42–43
FTE 42
net profit 42–43
productivity pyramid 43–44
wages and salaries 41
productivity levers 171–181
productivity pyramid 43–44, 213, 214
productivity wage quotient (PWQ) 5, 35, 214
of automatic cultures 33
of problematic cultures 20
of systematic cultures 29
of traumatic cultures 25
promise, of organization 45–48, 172–173, 214
Amazon (case study) 57
Blue Rocket accounting (case study) 173–174
clothing manufacturer (case study) 50–51
Crystal Ski (case study) 46
Dyson (case study) 55
GB rowing team (case study) 52
I know model 49–51
known model 54–56
Kodak (case study) 49
motor garage (case study) 53–54
Ratners jewellers (case study) 56–57
they know model 53–54
we know model 51–53
who knows? model 48
prototyped process 112–115, 135, 125

Q

quality issues 187
quick wins 184, 185, 186

R

Ratners jewellers 56–57
recognition 108
remove me team members 89–90
case study 90–91
management of 106
Retail Price Index 68
Revson, Charles 46–47
reward schemes 106, 108–109
Richer, Julian 103
risk gauging 132

S

Sands, Nora 104–105
Senge, Peter 200
service business 190–191
Simone, Ralph 199
skills gap, and productivity, 8–9, 15
'slow down to go faster' concept 199, 202, 205
software implementations 125
spreadsheets 136–137, 138
staff, *see* people
stagnant pricing 67–69
structured management practices 12
structured problem-solving approach 23–24
systematic cultures
audiovisual start-up (case study) 30–31
and prioritization 189–191
of productivity 29–32, 189–191

T

tacit processes 115–118, 135–136, 125
team members, *see* people
technical debt 127
they know model 53–54, 61
train me team members 94, 96–97
case study 97–98
management of 107
traumatic cultures

apprenticeship training company (case study) 26–27
distributor (case study) 28
and prioritization 186
of productivity 25–28, 186
Unblock Audit 118, 119–120, 143
collector, becoming a 163
facilitators 143–144, 163, 214
global pharmaceutical (case study) 166–167
historical data 159
knowing what to expect 152–154
metal recycling (case study) 156
multi-discipline consultancy (case study) 151–152
naive style 144–145
new ideas and change 161–165
opportunity quantification 154–157
possibilities, exploring 159–161
PR company (case study) 154–155
recording the discovery 165
scheduling time 150–152
speaking with relevant team members 149–150
and spreadsheets 158–159
structured conversation 145–148
uncertainty, overcoming 157
updating the map 165–166

V

valued pricing 75–80
VAT (Value Added Tax) 3–4
Vistage network 200
visual stories, and change 203–207

W

wages and salaries 41
we know model 51–53, 60–61
Whitehurst, Jim 19
who knows? model 48, 59–60
Workerbee recruitment 178–179
Wynter, Barnaby 81

A quick word from Practical Inspiration Publishing...

We hope you found this book both practical and inspiring – that's what we aim for with every book we publish.

We publish titles on topics ranging from leadership, entrepreneurship, HR and marketing to self-development and wellbeing.

Find details of all our books at: www.practicalinspiration.com

Did you know...

We can offer discounts on bulk sales of all our titles – ideal if you want to use them for training purposes, corporate giveaways or simply because you feel these ideas deserve to be shared with your network.

We can even produce bespoke versions of our books, for example with your organization's logo and/or a tailored foreword.

To discuss further, contact us on info@practicalinspiration.com.

Got an idea for a business book?

We may be able to help. Find out more about publishing in partnership with us at: bit.ly/PIpublishing.

Follow us on social media...

 @pip_talking

 @practicalinspiration

 @piptalking

 Practical Inspiration Publishing